Life Coaching for Writers

An Essential Guide to
Realising your Creative Potential

Life Coaching for Writers

An Essential Guide to Realising your Creative Potential

Sarah-Beth Watkins

COMPASS BOOKS

Winchester, UK
Washington, USA

First published by Compass Books, 2014
Compass Books is an imprint of John Hunt Publishing Ltd., Laurel House, Station Approach,
Alresford, Hants, SO24 9JH, UK
office1@jhpbooks.net
www.johnhuntpublishing.com
www.compass-books.net

For distributor details and how to order please visit the 'Ordering' section on our website.

Text copyright: Sarah-Beth Watkins 2013

ISBN: 978 1 78279 239 0

A CIP catalogue record for this book is available from the British Library.

Design: Stuart Davies
www.stuartdaviesart.com

Printed and bound by CPI Group (UK) Ltd, Croydon, CR0 4YY

We operate a distinctive and ethical publishing philosophy in all
areas of our business, from our global network of authors to
production and worldwide distribution.

CONTENTS

Chapter 1 - The Write Focus   1

How Can Life Coaching Help Me as a Writer?   2

The Creative Juggler   3

Your Creative Purpose   3

Myriad Ideas   4

The Four Stages of Emotional Commitment   5

Visualisation   6

Mind Maps   7

Chunking it Down   8

Creating Your Writing Ritual   8

How Do Other Writers Start Their Day?   9

Chapter 2 - Setting your Writing Goals   11

Your Values and Passions   11

Setting Your Goals   13

Smart Thinking   14

Time Management   15

The Key to Motivation   17

Using a Visual Board   18

Creating Your Vision Statement   18

Picture Your Book   19

Write its Review   20

Compelling Futures   20

Chapter 3 - Freedom to be Creative   22

Believe in Your Inner Writer   22

Getting Rid of your Gremlins   23

Stopping the NATS   24

Your States of Mind   26

Overcoming Obstacles   27

Clearing Writer's Block   28

The Anti-Ritual   29
Don't Succumb to Procrastination   30
Changing Perspective   30
Dealing with Creative Anxiety   31
Using the FEAR mnemonic   32

Chapter 4 - A Writer's Life   **34**
The Writing Day   34
Daily Intentions   35
Managing a Schedule   36
The Call of Chores   37
Balancing it All   38
Dealing with Deadlines   39
Maintaining Momentum   39
Supporting Yourself   40
Making Others Understand Your Calling   41
Communication and Making Contacts   42
Embracing the Marketplace   43

Chapter 5 - Crossing Genres   **45**
Fiction v. Non-fiction   45
Changing Direction   46
Believing in New Projects   46
Managing Transitions   48
Is It Worth It?   49
Accomplishing Change   50
A Positive Story   51
Other Ways to Support Yourself Financially as a Writer 52
Giving up the Day Job   53

Chapter 6 - Looking after Yourself   **55**
Now Relax   55
Stress Management Techniques   56
Affirmations and Check-ins   58

Daily Gratitudes   59
Get Exercising   60
Dealing with Limiting Beliefs   61
How to Take Care of Your Writing Self   61
Avoiding Burnout   62

Chapter 7 - Successes and Rejections   **64**
You Can Do It – and You Have Done!   64
Celebrating Success   65
Congratulating your Creative Self   66
Fear of Success   67
It's not Failure   68
Dealing with Rejection   70
Planning for the Future   71

Chapter 8 - When the Going gets Tough   **73**
Getting it Down on Paper   73
Reframing the Issue   73
Using Diaries   74
Free-flowing Ideas   75
Creating Dialogue to Deal with Issues   76
The Power of Poetry   76
Listen to Your Dreams   77
Therapy Letters   78
A Letter to the Self   79
Taking a Break   79
Turning to Nature   81
Dusting Down and Clearing Out   81
Reviewing Your Goals   82
Seeking Help   83

Chapter 9 - Ways of Moving Forward   **85**
Maintaining a Writer's Momentum   85
Info Gathering   86

Educating Yourself   87
Online Support   87
Networking   88
Writing Groups – Yes or No?   89
Keeping your Creative Mind Active   91
Coaching Others   92
Taking an Active Role in a Writer's Organisation   93

Chapter 10 - Resources for the Writer's Mind   **94**
Websites for Writers   94
Organisations   95
Writing Courses   95
Writing Prompts   96
Critique Sites   97
Word Games   97
Competitions   98
Events   99
Social Media   100
Promoting Your Work   100

Further Reading   **101**
Contacting the Author   102

Appendix - Contributors   **103**

Chapter 1

The Write Focus

When I was at school, I wanted to be a librarian. I did my work experience in the local library and I just loved being surrounded by books on a daily basis. The career guidance teacher told me I would have to spend at least four years at university to follow my dream. Well that's not happening, I told her, I need a job not more education.

I never once linked my love of books to thinking of writing as a career path. My Granddad was always telling me I had a great imagination and I should be writing books but at sixteen, all I was writing was my diary. I still have it and believe me, that's something that will never see an editor's table.

It might not have occurred to me because I didn't spend much time in my English classes. I was always out in the corridor, sent out for talking too much, and awaiting the wrath of the Headmaster who got so used to seeing me there, he just used to shake his head and walk on. I wasn't bad at English, I just wasn't very good and I know I'm not the only one.

Simon Whaley, author of *The Positively Productive Writer*, says in the introduction of his book, 'Do I have a degree in writing? No. Did I get a good grade in my English O level? No (I scraped through with a C grade, which in those days was the lowest pass.)'

So it seems that not all writers start out with any inkling that they are going to be writers and the school system isn't a true reflection of a writer's skills which of course is good news to all those writers out there that aren't too proud of their English grades.

But somewhere along the line, I decided that writing was what I really wanted to do. I wanted to write articles, books, novels – anything and everything but I didn't know where to start and I didn't know what to focus on.

As a life and creativity coach, I see this problem come up time and time again for writers who want to make writing a career choice and not just beginners; writers who want to try a new genre, writers who are trying to escape a day job, writers who are making a living but want to write something completely different. I found life coaching a great way of helping me to focus on my own writing as well as helping others to focus on theirs.

How Can Life Coaching Help Me as a Writer?

Life coaching is about finding your focus, delving deep within yourself to find out where you want to go with your life and seeing what needs to change in order for you to fulfil your life's dreams. It looks at where you are in the present and where you want to be in the future. It's a journey of self-discovery with achievable goals manifested. Life coaching looks at your life in a holistic way and helps you to plan for success and to build your life around your goals.

Coaching can help you to be a better writer. Not because it's going to wave a wand over your creative skills and instantly give you the best literary skills in the country but because it will help you to clear out the clutter, get rid of unwanted negative thoughts and free you up to concentrate on the writing that is important to you, the writing that you want to focus on.

Coaching has its roots in enabling sports trainers to encourage their students to perform better. Creativity coaching is a relatively new field that helps writers and other creative people to move forward on their chosen path. It's not therapy or counselling but a way of assessing yourself in the present and moving yourself towards a positive future. Of course, there are many life coaches and creativity coaches that can help you as a client but you can also coach yourself with the many tips and exercises that this book contains. We'll look at life coaching, neuro-linguistic programming (NLP) and cognitive behavioural therapy (CBT) techniques that can really help you and your writing ambitions.

The Creative Juggler

Writers are jugglers. They have thoughts about new projects, half finished pieces of work, research to do and publishers to talk to about proposals. From having original ideas to selling them to the appropriate marketplace, there is a lot going on in a writer's life.

And this is as well as the everyday stuff that has to be dealt with. Not everyone can be creative all of the time. Writers may have a day job that takes time and energy, children that need their love and attention or elderly relatives that need care. Life throws up obstacles and challenges that we have to face and moments when we doubt ourselves and our writing abilities. It all conspires against a writing career but that's where life coaching can help.

The trick is to make time for your writing regardless of all the other demands in your life. This can be hard to do if you don't have a focus. If you just think I'll spend a couple of hours on Saturday morning doing my creative thing but you don't specify to yourself what that is, you might spend the hour thinking of a short story you could start on, a screenplay that you feel would be just the thing directors are looking for or some research you could do for a new book but you won't actually get started. You won't knuckle down to your creative work and before you know it your time has gone with nothing to show for it.

Your Creative Purpose

One of the best ways to achieve your creative goal is to focus your mind with a creative purpose visualisation. This will help you to hone in on what you really want to do. You can do this at any stage in your writing career but it is especially useful when you are in between writing projects and aren't sure what to focus on next.

Pick a quiet time when you can relax without interruption. Turn off the phone, close the door and sit in a comfortable position or if you prefer, find a space outside where you feel peaceful and can concentrate without distraction.

Close your eyes and imagine yourself in a very plush hotel. You have been asked to attend a prestigious award-giving event. You are sitting with friends and family right at the front, waiting for someone to come to the podium. When they do, they announce the main award. As everyone starts applauding, the award winner comes to the podium. It is you in the future!

Let your mind imagine what you say next as you give your acceptance speech.

- What is the award for?
- What have you achieved?
- How does this make you feel?

Feel yourself accepting the award, thanking the people who have come here especially to see you and absorb your accomplishment for a few moments.

You may be surprised at your creative purpose. When I did this myself, I imagined I was receiving an award for a historical book. I've written a couple of historical articles and I do love history but I never thought that this would resurface as something I would be truly proud of and would really want to do.

Myriad Ideas

I collect ideas and the historical novel is just one of them. I have lots and lots of ideas for all different types of writing. I might never actually decide on some of these ideas and go all the way with them but I collect them nevertheless for when I need inspiration. The problem with this is that sometimes I find I can't settle on any one idea. I can't find my focus.

If this sounds like you then I have one way of narrowing down the field for you and it's as simple as using a rating system. List your ideas on a sheet of paper then go through them first to see what is doable right now. Not when you have new technology to help you, have bought supplies or have done the research – what could you start today?

This will narrow down your list measurably. Then ask yourself – how passionate am I about this idea? Give each item a rating from one to ten. Cross out anything below a seven. If you're not passionate about your project then you won't motivate yourself to complete it. You only want to start something that you can focus on and if you are passionate about it, it will take up your thoughts and goad you into action.

This should leave you with only one or two glowing ideas. It's ok to focus on more than one idea if you are able to – many writers work on several projects at any one time. I often have a few projects on the go at once but these are ones that I allot time to and know that I will be able to focus on and complete. It might be a short article, a book synopsis and the current manuscript that I am working on but each has its place and time.

The Four Stages of Emotional Commitment

Professor Costas Markides of the London Business School developed a strategy for engaging business people in new ideas, decisions or plans. It can be adapted for use by writers to help you to focus on your desired project by working through the four stages of emotional commitment. The stages are:

- I know
- I understand
- Yes, I think I can
- I will

The first stage 'I know' is about arming yourself with as much information about your project as possible. So if you want to write a historical novel, you know what research you want to do, which publisher you will aim your work at and you have thought about a time scale for your work.

The second stage 'I understand' helps you to think of what this writing project will mean to you. Why do it? What will it bring you? How will it make you feel? When you understand the significance of your idea then you can decide whether this is the focus you need to take.

'Yes, I think I can' is the third stage and this comes when you have weighed up your project and you consider whether you can commit to it fully and see it through to its end. The transition from this stage to the next seems to be the hardest for writers. Like I said before, I have many ideas so I can get to this stage with a handful of projects that I know I can do but will I actually do them?

And this brings us to the decision, the decision to focus on that one project or a few if you can juggle them, but the ones you can and will focus on. The 'will' is so important here. Yes, you think you can but to have the will means to have the focus and to ultimately decide that you are going to see your creative work to completion. Not just start it or do a bit but see it through.

Visualisation

Visualisation is a really helpful tool that you can use to boost your self-esteem and to increase your confidence over the success of a new project. We often self-talk ourselves out of writing projects by thinking negatively about the outcome. We say things to ourselves like 'I don't think this is really going to work' or 'I don't think the world is ready for me to do this' and 'No one's going to like my writing'. This doesn't help us to focus. It doesn't help us to feel that this is the right project for us and that what we are doing is worthwhile.

You can use visualisation to see the success of your project in the future, to see yourself achieving and accomplishing your goal and this in turn will help you to focus on your writing as you work towards your goal.

As in the creative purpose section, find a quiet time and space and see yourself working on your writing project, see it coming to fruition and imagine the outcome – the finished piece and its reception. If you can imagine the outcome of your current project, it can help you to focus in on it as something you really want to achieve and complete.

Mind Maps

If you are still really stuck on what to focus on, you can try mind mapping or brainstorming. This can also help you to decide on what to focus on in more depth. First, take a piece of paper and write down your main idea.

Think of all the ways in which you could develop this idea. Take a coloured pen and add branches off of your main word to list in what ways this idea could be expanded. It doesn't matter how big or small, just add them all in.

Don't think too hard; just write down anything and everything that comes to mind. Let ideas surface and write them down. We are not looking for works of art, we are just generating a flow of ideas that you can take or leave once you have considered them later on. Here is your opportunity to write anything down you would like to focus on.

Leave your mind map for a few days then go back to it. Pick out the top three creative ideas you had. Now brainstorm each one. Think about how you can start working on your best idea. It could be that now you have a sudden burst of inspiration and are ready to start. If not, break your idea down into smaller steps. Are there things you can do to prepare yourself – like research, Internet browsing or reading a related book?

Chunking it Down

As a creativity coach, I advise writers to chunk their ideas down. This is a well tested NLP technique that can help you to make your writing seem more realistic and more doable. One of my clients recently told me that he had an idea for a book but it would be an in-depth scientific book that would mean a lot of research and he just didn't know where to start. I asked him to break down his idea into steps so he had a list that read something like – plan chapters, do research, write a proposal, get an expert to write the introduction, find quotes from the professionals, and so on. Then I asked him to take each one of these steps again and break it down. So for planning chapters, he would write chapter titles, work out the number of chapters, decide on the focus of each chapter, etc. I asked him to pick one and commit to it during the following week. He chose writing the chapter titles but this was enough of a smaller task to make him believe he could manage the whole project and within the week, he had actually planned out a chapter list, titles and the focus for each chapter. Sometimes starting a project can be the hardest task of all but by chunking down what seems to be an insurmountable body of work into manageable pieces, it can help you to focus on developing and ultimately completing that project.

Creating Your Writing Ritual

Once you have decided on your focus, the project you are going to undertake, you have the extra job of focusing on it at any given time. So you have those precious hours on Saturday mornings but if you sit there checking your Facebook page, stroking the cat and staring out of the window, it's still not going to be a productive session.

Many writers have a ritual that they go through before giving their complete attention to the work in hand. It could be lighting a candle, doing a visualisation or spending a few moments deep breathing to calm the mind. It could be chucking out the cat, drinking a cup of coffee whilst looking at yesterday's work or turning off the phone and turning on the computer. Whatever it is, it signals that now is the time to write.

Create your own ritual that tells you that this is your writing time. It's not for anything else. It's for focusing on your project. When the ritual is over, it's time for work.

How Do Other Writers Start Their Day?

When I asked around my writing colleagues how they settled down to focus on the task at hand, they came up with some illuminating stories. Sarah, a fiction writer, said, "I live near an old bookstore and they do the best coffee! I start my writing day by sitting amongst other writers and readers, notebook at the ready. I think about what I want to get done today and make any notes for plot points, characters or settings I want to include in my current story. Then I go home and with no excuses, turn on the computer and get started."

Claire has a different way. "I have children that need to go to school, a house that will need cleaning and animals to feed. Once they are done, I spend 15-20 minutes on yoga stretches and use deep-breathing to clear my mind. If I feel too energetic to sit and type, I turn on the digital recorder and talk my way around the house developing the next stage of my story as I pace about. I know I'll have to sit down to type at some point but I have to use up some energy first."

Suzanne Ruthven, author of *Life-Writes, The Country Writer's Craft, How To Write for the How-To Markets, The Pagan Writer's Guide* and *Horror Upon Horror: How to Write a Horror Novel* says, "First thing in the morning, I spend an hour in bed with a cup of tea to plan what's got to be done that day. If I don't have this 'thinking time', I find it very difficult to get started."

And Sarah Zama, a fantasy writer and illustrator, has an interesting way of starting her writing sessions. "All the main characters of my story have their own song. A song that for some reason makes me think of them. Before I start writing, I play the song connected to the character that will appear in that day's writing. It helps me get going in the right frame of mind."

Whatever way gets you in the writing mood, use it to focus on your intentions for the day.

Chapter 2

Setting Your Writing Goals

Once you have decided what to focus on, you can begin setting your goals. You can also do this on a regular basis like once a year or every six months to review what you have done and plan for what you want to do in the future. Goals come in all shapes and sizes so spend some time on working out the little and the large to really have your writing commitments fixed in your mind.

Your Values and Passions

First I'd like to ask you to think about your values and passions. I mentioned in chapter one that when you go through your current ideas you should rate them as to how passionate you are about them. I'm sure as a writer you are sick of hearing the adage: you should write what you know. It should really be: you should write what you are passionate about!

This doesn't really happen when you are trying to make a living as a writer. I know I have had days when I've been asked to write an article and the thoughts of it are painful. I might know the subject and I might have written about it before but I just don't want to do it. I don't ever turn down a chance of publication so I sit at the computer and the minutes drag by as I try to get the article written.

Yet if I was to write a paragraph of my current fiction attempt or dabble with an article that I have a great idea for, the minutes fly by. When you are passionate about what you write, it doesn't seem like a chore but many writers have to write all sorts to get the bills paid and that's ok, as long as you still leave room for your passions.

One way of tapping into your passions is to write your

Love/Hate list. Take two pages in a notepad and write Love on the top of one and Hate on the top of the other then just freeflow words onto the pages. Passion isn't always positive. Your love list might contain some great ideas for things that you want to write about but what about your hate list? This can contain some real gems that you could turn into articles, first person pieces or use as the basis for character conflict in a story.

Your values are the essence of who you are and what is important to you. Values are sort of hard to pinpoint and can be abstract. We don't often think hey, what are my values? But you'll surely feel them when you try to write something that doesn't underpin your values. Writers often have great values like independence, creativity, freedom, freedom to be creative, self-expression and productivity and these are like the foundation that our goals are based upon. If we take on a project that doesn't allow us creative freedom, that stints our productivity, and dents our self-expression, then we feel it. We know that something is wrong yet we might not see that our values are at play. But when we are in agreement with our values, the choices we make leave us feeling fulfilled.

I say this because I know many writers don't always write what they want to and this can affect their goals. They say I'd really love to work on this or that but I'll have to do a, b and c first. I know we have to make a living, guys, but you can't keep compromising. At some point you have to say look this is my writing goal and I'm going to do it no matter if it takes a year or five years. This is the thing that will make me fulfilled and yeah, I'll do all the other bits but I'm making room for my ultimate writing goal starting now.

One of my clients writes stories. She is really successful in writing for women's magazines and although she still gets rejected at times, she's ok with that because she'll just bash out another story and it pays the bills. But what she really wants is to write is a screenplay. She'd love to write a script and see it produced but it's a long term commitment and one that might not pay off. Then again, it could pay off big time and make her a huge success and financially stable.

If you have writing goals that are there but are not ever worked upon, you will never know if they are going to pay off unless you do them. You can live your life with ifs and buts and maybes and never feel that joy of ultimate fulfilment, of writing what you are passionate about and what speaks to your values. So before you set your goals, just consider your values and passions, write with those in mind and unleash the creative potential that underpins your values and is unique to you.

Setting Your Goals

Let's talk long term, medium and short term goals. Or you could say in five years' time, a year's time and this week. Give each of your goal types a timeframe. This helps in planning ahead and gathering your thoughts. If like me, you have many writing projects in mind, it can help to portion them out and it will make insurmountable tasks seem much easier.

Take a big sheet of paper and divide it into three columns – long, medium and short. Then add underneath those headings your timeframe. Next, start going through your ideas and allocating them to their appropriate columns. Put your larger goals in the long term category. Say, for instance, you want to write a book. A long term goal could be its publication, a medium term goal is to write it and the short term goals break up that writing into manageable chapters or chunks.

My short term goals tend to be a weekly list of to-dos with a monthly overall goal list. It's the timeframe thing again! So for this month, I have to write at least three chapters of my book, do some research on Tudor history, write four articles, attend a conference, start building a new website and do three book reviews. So I start week one with write a chapter, write an article, write a book review, prepare conference speech notes, choose a website name and watch *The Tudors* (again!). They are my monthly goals broken into smaller pieces. I might not get it all done and then some will carry over to the next week but I'm en route to getting my monthly goals achieved.

These all build into the bigger picture of my medium goals that I set for a year. Most of my long term goals are more abstract like write more books or continue to write lifestyle articles but I do have one long finger project which is the writing of a historical novel. It's a huge undertaking and something I can't commit to right now but it can be a long term goal and I can build in some ways of working towards it by setting smaller goals like research or note-taking.

What long term projects do you have that you can start achieving by breaking them down in this way? Once you start work on them, however small, you'll feel a real sense of getting something achieved and you'll be delighted when you can tick off those smaller goals and know that you are well on the way to fulfilling your creative dreams.

Smart Thinking

Have you heard of SMART? Specific, measurable, achievable, relevant and timescaled. You can use these headings to set your goals. However, I prefer another method that has its origins in the GROW model designed by John Whitmore. This is the I-CAN-DO technique. Sounds much better, doesn't it?

- I is for investigate. What is important to you? What ideas for writing projects are floating around right now?
- C is for current. What is your current situation? Where do you currently stand as a writer? What are your previous successes?
- A are your aims. What do you want to achieve? What writing project means the most to you right now?
- N is the number of options, routes or paths you can take to

achieve your aims. Narrowing it down, what route could you take to achieve your current writing goal?

- D is for the date by which time you will have this particular writing project finished.
- O is for the outcome. What do you hope to achieve ultimately? And how will you know when this is done?

You can use this at any time but especially to clarify your thinking about one goal in particular. It can narrow down your thinking, helping you to settle on a goal that you will give a completion date for and answer what you hope to achieve by doing this particular project.

Time Management

Time is one of the hardest things for a writer to find. It's something that I have talked to a lot of writers about and it comes up time and time(!) again in creative coaching sessions. Finding time for your writing is about prioritising what's important to you and letting something go that can just wait. For instance, I have decided that my writing time this afternoon is just for writing this book and nothing else. The washing machine can wait, the dinner can be a takeaway and I walked the dog this morning! Right now is writing time and I will not be distracted!

Sometimes you just have to say no to all the other things that you think you need to do. Notice I say *think* you need to do. Do you really have to do them? Are they all so important that they get priority over writing? Can other arrangements be made for someone else to help out, do the chores or collect the kids? Save your time to write.

Time management means being creative about finding time and recognising your time stealers. Time stealers are those things that you do that aren't really necessary. Like watching two hours of soaps in the evening or surfing the Internet for three hours instead of just using it for research. Now I'm not saying stop everything you like doing and write but if you find that you don't have enough time for your writing, is there something you can give up? Can you have a day off on Sunday and watch all the soaps then thus giving you writing time in the evenings? Can you limit your Internet use to an hour only of research a day and save the online shopping for Saturday?

Have a think about what uses up your time. One suggestion is to write a time diary. Keep it for a week and just note down on an hourly basis what you were doing. You can fill this in at the end of the day if you don't want to keep opening up your notebook. Look to see where time could be saved and then put your time to better writing use.

What you will find are lots of little time gaps; say when you're waiting for a train, are queuing in the doctor's surgery or are waiting in the car for the kids to come out of school. We spend a lot of our time waiting and it's an important gap that can be utilised for better effect. You might think that the gap is too small to do anything productive in but try out some of these tips:

- Print off your latest story or article and have it with you to edit while you're waiting
- Take a book with you for research
- Work out a character biography
- Start the chapter list of a non-fiction book
- Listen to an audio-book or poetry reading for inspiration
- Write down book or article ideas
- Keep a writing guide handy for information and advice on something you are currently working on

You can fill all the little gaps with things that support your writing even if you don't have time to write pages of text. Always carry something to do with you or leave stuff in the car for when you find you have waiting time and you want to use it productively.

The Key to Motivation

So you've got goals but what actually makes you sit in front of the computer, get a notebook out or finish that piece of writing that's been bugging you for ages? Motivation! But what is motivation? Well, we feel motivated to achieve our goals by thinking of their outcome. It could be recognition, money, security, achievement, prestige or power but it could also be personal growth, self-esteem or independence. What makes you feel like you want to write?

Some writers find this hard to define because writing is so much a part of them. When I asked Suzanne Ruthven, what motivated her to write, she said "An inbuilt urge that's been with me since I was a kid. It was all I'd ever wanted to do and I've now nearly 40 titles under my belt."

Deborah Durbin, author and journalist, says "For me it's the joy of sharing information with other people, whether it's passing on my skills as a journalist and writer in my book, *So You Want To Be A Freelance Writer?*, or making people laugh with my novels. Money also motivates me. It means that someone values my work enough to pay me for it."

Another writer, Nik Morton, author of *Write a Western in 30 Days*, told me "I've been writing for over 40 years, and selling since 1971. I cannot not write. Motivation for each story, article or novel is to tell a story that interests me, whether that's sci-fi, fact, spy, romance, horror, western, fantasy or erotica."

Sarah Zama, a writer and illustrator, told me, "I know this may sound melodramatic, but writing is just something I need to do in my life, just like wearing clothes. Writing helps me drain the tension of the day off me. It helps me think out things and sort them out.

And then caring about my characters, seeing them going through their troubles and coming out of it, stronger and possibly happier, is just plain fun. It's good. It makes me feel good."

Some writers don't need to be motivated to write because writing is such a core element of their being. It's an urge, an impulse, a need that has to be realised but they do need to be in a motivating environment to get started. I'm sure you've read articles about making your creative space or having a writing corner all of your own and you will have some sort of set-up at home but is it inspirational? Does it motivate you to write?

Using a Visual Board

One thing you can do to liven up your writing space is to adorn it with a vision board and your statement. This is a great technique you can use that will give you something else to do creatively and can fill a gap when you are feeling unproductive or blocked. Say you have the goals of writing a fantasy saga, having your own garden office and lecturing on creative writing. You can build a vision board that reminds you of your goals and have it prominently placed in your writing area to goad you on and inspire you to achieve them. You can add in quotes you've read, inspirational tips and pictures of anything that motivates you to write.

Buy a cheap cork board or make your own with a couple of cork tiles from the hardware store. Cut out pictures from magazines, postcards you've collected, drawings, images off the Internet; anything that makes you feel good and speaks to your inner writer. Also choose images that represent your goals; a dragon for a fantasy book, a picture of an office space, a flyer that advertises a creative writing lecture – use tickets, adverts, flyers, quotes, writing tips, a favourite author's name and use them all to make a collage that helps you to think of your goals. I have a friend who even attached a cheque she'd written for herself that signified the advance she hoped to get for her first book!

Creating Your Vision Statement

Writing your vision is all about empowering yourself and having a statement that is unique to you in a prominent position near your work space. Vision statements are positive paragraphs that can reflect your values, your personality and your aims. Think of what you want to be and how you would like to be portrayed if success knocked on your door. What would you say of yourself?

You can add a vision statement to your vision board and use it to remind yourself just how wonderful and motivated you really are! You could write something like:

I am a writer who works to create pictures in people's minds. I write everyday regardless of how I feel, how much I procrastinate and how much I can't find inspiration. I am a writer and a creative person who can write and will always write. I am creating my own body of work that will be read by others. My words will reach across the globe.

The idea is to make your vision statement personal to you so that it will motivate you, inspire you and put a smile on your face so that when negative thoughts start creeping in, you can read your statement and it will boost your confidence, giving you that extra bit of faith in yourself and the knowledge that you will achieve your goals.

Picture Your Book

Making a visual board helps you to picture your goals and the writing you are going to do. Sometimes being able to see your writing as a finished project can spur you on to achieve your goals. To give yourself a break from writing and especially when the going gets tough, design your own book cover and add it to your vision board. I don't mean you have to get special design software and make the perfect cover on your computer. If you enjoy computer design then work away but otherwise find an image that appeals to you and add your title and name to it as a mock-up of a book cover. Seeing what your book may look like as a finished version can spur you on to getting that writing done and turn you into a published author.

Write its Review

You can even go as far as writing your own review! If you are working on a book or screenplay, try writing its review as a boost to your self-esteem. Imagine you open up the Sunday paper and there in amongst the arts and entertainment pages is a review of your work. And it's really good! Your writing is being lauded as the next best thing and you are the star of the moment. Write this review yourself, saying all the wonderful and inspiring things you just know people want to say about you! Pin this up on your vision board too and you will have a range of images and quotes that will inspire and motivate you to get those goals done!

Compelling Futures

This is a type of confidence boosting visualisation that can be used to check in with each of your goals to make sure that it's what you really want to do, that it's important enough to you and that its completion will make you feel fulfilled. It will also help you to picture the outcome of your goal which is especially useful when you are experiencing self-doubt and trying to talk yourself out of achieving it.

To make the visualisation of your future as vivid to you as possible, use what in NLP we call our representational systems. These are the way in which we view our world and how we engage our senses to do so.

So when you are imagining your future, like attending an award ceremony, being voted the best romance novelist, or giving a workshop based on your best-selling book, use all your senses to bring it alive. I tend to see everything visually but to the point that I don't take notice of sounds. Everyone has their own way of imagining things but step outside of your usual way to include sight, sound, touch, smell and taste to give your future substance. You might be able to see it in your mind but what do the canapés taste like, what background music is playing, how does it feel when another famous author slaps you on the back and a well-known personality shakes your hand?

Imagine your future in a positive way. See what all your goals can bring you. Feel the emotions that you will experience when your goals are achieved. Then you will not only be able to set your goals, you'll be able to envision a life where you have accomplished them – and are ready to achieve some more!

Chapter 3

Freedom to be Creative

We are our own worst enemies. We talk ourselves out of writing projects, we tell ourselves we won't ever get a piece of work finished and we hear an awful voice telling us to not even bother starting. No one is immune from self-doubt and negative thoughts. It happens to all writers whatever stage of their career they are at. But learning to stop thoughts in their tracks, disbelieving your gremlins and overcoming obstacles is part of being a writer and the more you do it, the better you get so that when you start to say to yourself 'I can't write this', you can shut that thought out and say 'oh yes, I can!'

Believe in Your Inner Writer

Let's start on a positive note first. Knowing why you want to be creative will help you to believe in yourself as a writer. Beliefs are our strongly held opinions, attitudes and convictions. Beliefs can be so strong they cause warfare, persecution and dissent. They can exert influence over our behaviour, thoughts and reactions but where do they come from?

Our beliefs start forming from the moment we are born. We gain them from our parents, caregivers, teachers and others who influence our lives. As we grow older, we challenge some beliefs and hold onto others. Beliefs can change but they can also be stubborn. What positive beliefs do you have in relation to yourself?

List five of those positive beliefs about yourself. Make them as bold and proud as they can be. I came up with – I am a fabulous cook. I am the most gorgeous woman in the world. I am kind, gentle and loyal. I am the best friend you could have. I am the greatest writer that ever lived.

Ok, so this may be completely over the top but I bet they made you smile. What are your beliefs? Do they make you smile? Write your list like mine. Boost your confidence. This is all about you. You can have the most positive beliefs about yourself. Notice my last sentence. Did you include being a writer on your list?

No? Then this is where to start. You need to have a positive belief in your inner writer, in your ability to be creative and in your aspiration to be the best in whatever form your writing takes. Even repeating the belief 'I am a writer' as a mantra several times a day will boost your confidence in your abilities. Narrow it down to your own specialist writing ability. Say 'I am a romance novelist', 'I am a short story writer', 'I am a non-fiction author' – whatever you want to be or are in the process of becoming. Telling your creative mind who you really are on a regular basis will invigorate and inspire your thinking. Unfortunately, beliefs are not always positive and the rest of this chapter will help you to deal with those times when negativity rears its ugly head.

Getting Rid of Your Gremlins

Did you know that Roald Dahl believed he had invented gremlins? In a brilliant biography written by Donald Sturrock, it tells the tale of how the world famous Dahl came up with a story about gremlins and tried to sell its film version to Disney. Unfortunately, it never went into production but whether your gremlins look like Disney characters or something more sinister, they need dealing with.

Who are your gremlins? They are the voices in your head that send you negative thoughts (see below) but they can actually have some basis in past experiences. It could be the voice of your old English school teacher, a parent, an editor, a partner or anyone who has disrespected your work, told you it's no good and has undermined your confidence in your writing.

Try to identify your gremlin. The next time you hear a disapproving voice in your head – think who this sounds like – is it someone you know or knew? Picture them and then tell them to go to hell! Honestly, you don't need to be listening to them anymore.

Some creative coaches recommend actually drawing a picture of your gremlin. If you enjoy art, it's a great way of putting a visual to that negative voice and you can make your gremlin as ugly and horrible as you want. Using this technique helps you to realise that your gremlins are unworthy of your attention and they need to be stopped. I tell my more visual clients to picture their gremlin and then lock them in a dungeon! Don't listen to them and don't let them out to negatively influence your thoughts.

Stopping the NATS

NATS are negative automatic thoughts. Or what I call nasty awful thoughts. They come from nowhere, are real downers and the more you try not to think them, the more they hum around your head like the gnats that they are. They can be your gremlins but they are worse than that. They are unbidden, annoying thoughts that tell you you're a rubbish writer, that you'll never succeed, that you should even stop trying and the thoughts just whirl round and round.

And I have found that writers that have completed at least one major project are particularly susceptible to them. Of course, beginners have fears and negative thoughts but I've talked to so many writers who have accomplished so much and then their NATS get the better of them. I know after I had my first book published that I went into a panic about only having one book in me. It was like maybe that's all I'd ever do and that's it. Published writers begin to create their own new identities and the fear of never being published again seems to be a recurring thought.

One of the easiest ways to stop negative thoughts is to

recognise them and change them. Say you are going about your daily chores and the little voices are randomly telling you things like you won't get that article finished in time, that that idea isn't worth pursuing and that the manuscript you sent out is going to be returned. Recognise it. Stop and say hey, that's negative now let's change that to a positive – I'll get that article done this afternoon, I'm going to do the research for that new idea, my manuscript is going to be accepted.

What we think is what we feel. This is a saying that cognitive behavioural therapy is based on. CBT teaches us not to block our thoughts but to test them for their truth. How do you know that you won't get your article done or that your manuscript will be returned? You don't – you're thinking of a negative outcome before it has happened. Sometimes this occurs because we base it on a previous experience so you think that your manuscript will be returned because it was returned before. If that was the case, no one's books would ever get published. If it comes back, it's time to review your work, take on board any feedback and try a different publisher. But you don't know that it will, it's out of your control and thinking negatively about it isn't going to change the outcome.

Writers all have different ways of stopping negative thoughts. Deborah Durbin, author and journalist, says, "I try not to read negative reviews! Thankfully the majority of my reviews have been five stars and have all been lovely, but there are a couple of negative ones out there, but that comes with the job. You're never going to please everyone, so don't try to. I also try to keep everything in perspective and tell myself it's not the end of the world if someone doesn't like my work, or an editor doesn't give me a commission. There are worse things happening out there in the world."

Krystina Kellingley, author and editor of Axis-Mundi Books, says, "If I think there is really room for improvement in something I've written, I edit it until I think otherwise. I also ask people I can trust to tell me the truth when I ask them what they think. If all else fails I just get on with it anyway."

Sarah Zama, writer and illustrator, says, "Negative thoughts like 'I can't possibly sort out the project I'm working on', or 'My writing hopelessly sucks, how could anyone ever be willing to read this', or 'I'm making a mess of all the characters'. These kinds of thoughts? I tell myself: look, there are plenty of things you could rather be doing, like going for a walk, watching a movie, read someone else's writing, cleaning your house. If you think writing is not worth doing, just do one of the other things instead. Never happened so far.

"I also like reading quotations from professional writers because I often find them inspiring. One of my favourite is from E.L. Doctorow who says, 'It's like driving a car at night. You never see further than your headlights, but you can make the whole trip that way.' Or Peter De Vries who said, 'I write when I'm inspired, and see to it that I'm inspired at nine o'clock every morning.' Or also Stephen Covey who commented, 'The main thing is to keep the main thing the main thing.' They are fun, but they are also inspiration."

Suzanne Ruthven, author and editor of Compass Books, has a more practical way of dealing with negative thoughts, "I sit and stare at the mountains for half an hour in the fresh air, or take the dogs out."

Sometimes a change of state can help you to banish those negative thoughts and get yourself back on track. Exercise and time out can do it but you can also change your state of mind.

Your States of Mind

In neuro-linguistic programming, we talk about states of mind with the aim of being able to change them when they are negative. At any given time, you are always in a state – that is your emotional, mental, physical and neurological elements combine to make you feel like how you are feeling, creating your current state of mind. For example, you may feel sad, angry, or frustrated about a writing project that doesn't seem to be going anywhere. The problem with being in a negative state is that it is not conducive to a successful and productive writing session.

The good news is you can change your state. One way of doing this is through a technique called anchoring. What you need to do is recognise the anchors that put you in a good state. What makes you feel happy about your work? What puts you in a good writing mood? Anchors can be as simple as the smell of freshly brewed coffee, birdsong outside of your window or the purr of the cat as it nestles on your lap ready for you to start writing. Think about what makes you feel good about your writing. It could be the memory of seeing your first book in print or reading an outstanding review. As I've said before you can have these things displayed in your writing area to trigger positive feelings but you can also return to positive, constructive thinking by triggering your mind to think of feel-good states. Once you recognise the anchors that make you feel happy about your writing, you can recall them at any time when your mood has dipped. It will change your state of mind and get you back into a writing mood.

Overcoming Obstacles

Sometimes we find it difficult to move ahead with our goals. There are obstacles in our way but we can't see them clearly or hesitate with trying to get rid of them. One client told me that he just wasn't happy with any of his stories. He'd written loads of them but they always changed from what he had originally set out to write and he didn't feel this was normal. I reassured him that it was perfectly normal for something you are writing to change beyond its original conception. We talked around this issue for a while before I realised that what was actually under-lining his feelings about his stories was a fear of sending them out to an editor. He dreaded feedback so was already telling himself his stories were no good. He'd put in place an obstacle that would severely affect his chances of publication.

Do you put any obstacles in your own way? Think of a goal that is proving hard to achieve and consider whether you are putting obstacles before you. They may be internal such as my client had or they may be external such as not having enough time, needing a new computer or anything else you can use as an excuse!

Then draw up an action plan for each obstacle. What can you do to change the situation? Use a critique group to look at your work before you send it out, get up an hour earlier in the morning, give your PC a check-up... whatever it takes to remove that obstacle, note it down and plan to do it. By giving your obstacle a name and clarifying what you can do to get rid of it, you shall overcome!

Clearing Writer's Block

Oh, writer's block – so much has been written about it, whole books, in fact. Some writers believe they suffer from it, others think it's just something we make up as an excuse for not writing. Whatever it is, it's not a disease, it's not fatal and it just means you are not putting pen to paper or fingers to the keyboard. You obviously need to ask yourself why. What is it that is stopping you from writing?

Writer's block is the name given to just about anything to do with *not* writing – a lack of ideas, the gap between projects, a story that's not working, the book that's stalled after the first two chapters. If your current project is stalled then ask yourself why and be honest. Maybe this isn't the book you were meant to write, maybe this article needs to be written from a different perspective, maybe you need to do more work on your characters. For whatever reason your writing has stopped, there is a solution to get it going again but that solution is within you. Remember in chapter two, I mentioned passion? If you are not passionate about a project, the likelihood is it will stall at some point because your heart's just not in it. What are you writing it for then?

Marilynn Hughes, publisher and author of several books including *Come to Wisdom's Door* and *Prelude to a Dream*, told me, "I take a look at my published books shelf and honestly critique it. It makes me realize that whether or not I'm in a writer's block right now, I have done good work before, and I will do good work again."

The Anti-Ritual

In chapter one, I talked about having a creative ritual that starts your day, signalling to you that it's time to start writing. If you are suffering from writer's block, can't get started on a new project or are feeling bereft and idea-less after completing a major piece of work, a ritual might not help. You could go through your routine and then still sit with no clear thoughts or aim of where to go. Sometimes the anti-ritual can help.

I've just watched a documentary about creativity that proved that the brain starts to work creatively when it is doing mundane tasks. Doing nothing doesn't help and doing something taxing doesn't work. You need to keep your brain active but just enough so creativity can creep in and strike you with inspiration.

Try the anti-ritual. Do things differently for a couple of days. Change your routine and add in something new. New experiences can create new neural pathways in our minds so visit that place you've been meaning to research, have coffee with a writing friend in a different cafe, clear out your office space and update your vision board. Keep your mind open to new writing ideas but take a break and do something that you wouldn't usually do.

You could try writing at different times. If you're a morning person and you usually sit at the computer first thing. Leave that, go off for the day and see if writing in the evening gets your cognitive bits working again. I do the simple thing of not sitting at the computer and staring at a blank space but going out, walking the dog or taking a trip to the shops, and then sitting with pen and paper. I really find the computer frustrating when the words are not flowing so I grab a notebook and curl up on a comfy sofa to see what flows from the pen.

If you can change your routine for a day or two, it will refresh your need to get back to your current writing and also provide you with new thoughts about what other goals you hope to achieve.

Don't Succumb to Procrastination

As I was writing the title to this section, it reminded me of an article I read recently that stated that procrastination is actually needed in a writer's life to allow downtime and time for the brain to start thinking of new creative ideas. That's all well and good but when the brain stays in procrastination mode and doesn't go any further then you're in trouble.

Procrastination is by its definition to delay or postpone something. It's still going to be there when you've finished the chores, had a fifth cup of tea or wandered aimlessly round the house trying to find something else to do. It's just delaying the inevitable. If you find yourself procrastinating, you can set it a time limit. Allow yourself procrastination time, half an hour or an hour, then get to work. At this stage, you know you are a writer and you have a good idea of what you are going to write so putting it off inevitably isn't going to help you achieve your goals. By allowing yourself a certain amount of faffing time, you can say that's done now and now it's time to start writing.

Changing Perspective

If you're finding it hard to settle down to writing, it might be that you need a change of perspective. Are you looking at your work from the wrong point of view? In a workshop that I gave to fiction writers, I asked them to rewrite their first paragraphs from another character's point of view to see if that helped their writing to flow or gave them a different perspective on their story. For some writers, that was enough to take their writing on a different path.

Take an article that you are writing from a first person viewpoint, will it be better from an expert's point of view? Or that fiction book you are writing that might actually work better as fact? Try looking at your work from a different perspective and it might reveal another path that your writing could take that will actually make it easier and more appealing to you to write.

Dealing with Creative Anxiety

There is another form of negative thinking that affects us writers and its not to do with writing! It's the kind of anxiety that creeps up when you have to do something else like give a talk, lecture a group of students, do a radio interview or even appear on the TV!

Writers have other elements to their writing life that I'm sure you are aware of like promoting your work, selling yourself to an editor and cold-calling magazines with ideas. They come with their own anxieties and challenges.

When you have to do something that doesn't come naturally to you or makes you feel uncomfortable, take a few minutes to do a positive visualisation of the outcome. See yourself giving that interview, delivering that workshop and talking to that editor and visualise it all going well, in fact, going brilliantly. Consider the best possible outcome and then plan for it.

Preparation is key for allaying those nerves and getting you through anxious moments. Rehearse your talks and speeches. Take key notes with you. Soothe yourself with a cup of chamomile tea and a few drops of Rescue Remedy beforehand and keep those positive thoughts foremost in your mind. Don't over think the situation but instead turn your thoughts to where this could take you. You might get commissioned to write a series of articles on the basis of a call, someone that sees you give a speech might invite you to their writer's weekend workshops, a radio interview could lead to better publicity for your book – these are all positive outcomes that will build your career as a writer and give you the freedom to be more creative.

Using the FEAR Mnemonic

I love this – False Expectations Appearing Real. I'm a coward when it comes to tests at the doctor or a visit to the dentist but invariably it is never as bad as it seems. This mnemonic reminds me that I'm making up a worst case scenario that may appear real but isn't actually going to happen.

It's great to use for things that seem scary in your writing life like a first book signing, a first workshop, a conference speech or a meeting with your editor. If your imagination goes into overdrive and has you tripping up, forgetting your words, collapsing in a faint and throttling an argumentative editor, you can try using this. Saying the mnemonic can remind you that you are making up what may happen. You don't know what is going to happen in your future and there is really no point in trying to predict how badly something you're asked to do as a writer is going to turn out.

If you're a really positive person, you might just jump at every opportunity that comes your way and see them in a brilliant light. And that's great – go for them! But if like me, you over think everything to the point of actually saying 'No, I can't do that', then you need to convince yourself that you can. So many opportunities are lost by writers who just feel a little scared, not up to the challenge or afraid of trying something new. Because we talk ourselves out of it.

Next time you are asked to do something new, say yes and use the FEAR mnemonic when your brain starts saying oh no, oh no.

Let yourself think of the worst case scenario and then ask yourself, is that really a possibility? If you think it might happen, say like forgetting your words, then plan for that. It probably won't happen but take cue cards or a written speech with you just in case. If you think you'll trip up – I actually did this in front of an audience of hundreds and survived! – think how you'll laugh it off and make a joke of it. And as for your editor – they are human too – and throttling helps no one!

Overcoming obstacles, working through fear and dealing with negative thoughts are a part of everyone's lives but for writers they take on a dimension that can seriously affect productivity and creativity. Tell your gremlins to shut up, stop those negative thoughts and feel free to be the brilliant writer that you know you are.

Chapter 4

A Writer's Life

What does a writer's life look like? For everyone who makes a living by putting words to paper, it's different. You may have to balance a day job with your writing time, juggle a young family with your creative sessions or you might have a full writing day but isn't it fascinating to find out how other writers manage their time? Although I've been writing for many years now, I'm always interested to find out how other writers live their lives and manage to work creatively.

The Writing Day

Every writer has a different way of organising their day. I start with the small bits like emails, short articles, Facebook and Twitter updates and then head on to the bigger stuff. This usually means that my solid writing session comes in the afternoon. In the evening, I read and research, fill in my journal and check my to-do list.

Sarah Zama has to fit in her writing around her job in a bookstore. She says, "Because I work in the afternoons, I always write in the mornings. One hour, one hour and a half on a lucky day. Before cooking lunch. I'd love to be able to write in the evenings, as some of my friends do, because that would give me more time. But as hard as I've tried, I've never been able to produce anything decent in the nights."

Melinda Feeney told me about her writing day. "Get up, check out emails etc., write, stare at it, delete, write it again. I find myself reading my chapters over and over, playing it out in my mind, watching the characters and even sometimes becoming the characters to make their actions authentic. It may appear I sit and do nothing, but inside my head there is a lot of action. I don't think I could write if I skipped this part."

Deborah Durbin has a family to manage around her writing time. "Once my daughters have gone to school and college and my husband has gone to work, I do a quick tidy of the house, then turn my laptop on and check my emails, Amazon rankings and website for any messages. If I'm working to a deadline for a magazine or newspaper I will work on that first, but if I'm working on my novel then I will reread what I last wrote and jot down what I plan to write next. With novels I find I work better by writing by hand in a notebook, often on the sofa with day time telly in the background. I'll then transfer what I've written to the computer in the evening. I always go out for lunch and then continue for an hour or so before I pick up my youngest daughter at 3.15pm. I start again once everyone has been fed and watered and settled down for the evening."

Marilynn Hughes says, "There is no typical day. But I do start every day with writing first. Because I now have so many websites to manage and technical issues going on, if it is a writing day, I write first. Because it is your creative energies that dissipate first. I can always do that assembly line stuff like SEO and working on technical difficulties after. But writing inspiration cannot be reproduced, use it first."

Your writing day is what you make it and there is no right way of organising it. There is no great writer routine that you have to follow or precise way of doing things and there is great freedom in that. Your writing day can take many different shapes and if you find one way is not working for you then try another. Create your perfect writing time whether you have a day job, other responsibilities or chores to meet. Picture your ideal writing day and work towards achieving it.

Daily Intentions

To start your day well, you can set your intentions. I once reviewed a great little book by Tony Burroughs, *Get What You*

Want: The Art of Making and Manifesting Your Intentions. In it, he fully explains the process for manifesting what you truly want to achieve and how we can start each day anew by making fresh intentions. I think this can really apply to your writing day. As you wake each morning, you can set your daily intentions. I don't mean your to-do list or your goals although they can be a part of the thoughts you put out into the world. Intentions are broader, they connect you with the world around you and underline your need to write and your belief in yourself as a writer. You might say something like:

- I intend that I am letting go of negative beliefs regarding my writing.
- I intend that I am writing words that will speak to people.
- I intend that I own my creative process.

Whatever you intend, you are asking the universe to manifest it for you. It's like putting out your positive thoughts and being open to accepting that you can achieve your full writing potential. What better way to start the day!

Managing a Schedule

Some writers have a more practical way of getting their writing day underway. The writer, Nik Morton, says, "I maintain a schedule of work, using a spreadsheet. Admittedly, at times of high word-count towards the end of a book or short story, I may juggle time, but normally it's healthier to have a life outside writing too and switch off the computer." Nik works well balancing his writing life with his personal and to manage his working schedule, he uses a spreadsheet, something I never thought of doing before.

Ever read those articles in writing magazines that give you the day in the life of a writer? I love them because I think for one, I look to see if I share any similarities (well, I must be a writer then!) and for another, I also look out for ways of doing something differently or new so that my writing day feels refreshed or maybe just evolving. The only time that I rigidly stick to a schedule is when I'm writing a book and then it's a chapter by chapter process.

Deborah Durbin works in a similar way. She says, "I have three daughters, four dogs, one husband and a rabbit, so I don't tend to stick to a strict schedule and it all depends on what I'm working on. If I have a commission with a deadline, that takes priority, but I tend to work best in the evening when everyone is settled. I always say; if you only have a spare 30 minutes, use it to write. You can get a lot written in that time and over the course of a week you can easily write a chapter. Do that every month and within six months you will have your book written."

The Call of Chores

Yep, they do call especially when I am procrastinating and even when I have my schedule down to a tee. When I'm writing a book, I must have the cleanest house ever because I so need to hoover, polish and do laundry before ever sitting down at the computer. Talking to other writers, especially female ones, I detect a need to get the house in order before any serious writing can occur.

I recently had a week where three days were taken up with chores, running the kids around, going to appointments, talking to the bank manager, etc. and it absolutely threw me. When I finally got a day in which to write, it was like a huge sigh of relief. Sometimes you have to battle to put those chores aside and regain your writing time. I said to myself right since this week is not overly productive, I'll get everything out of the way so that next week can be mega-productive!

So sometimes chores do have to be scheduled in – unfortunately. Unless you are rich and have other people to do them for you. Saying that, there are ways of delegating chores, cutting corners on them and getting other people's support so that you can minimise the amount you have to do. After all, you do need time to be a writer too!

Balancing it All

What happens with us writers is that we all have to balance our lives with our writing careers. We are the ultimate creative jugglers keeping the balls of life, writing and future projects all up in the air at once. We have to pick and choose when we let one drop and when to concentrate on another trick.

Sarah Zama says, "It may seem hard sometimes, you may think there are so many things asking for your attention other than writing. It's easy to put it off 'because there's something more important to do right now' but in fact it isn't all that hard.

"Some three years ago I took part in the online novel writing challenge, NaNoWriMo. The challenge is writing the first draft of a novel of at least 50k words in just 30 days. I did it and won it, and I realised that, although it seems so many words, in fact you only need to write a little piece of it every day, which is entirely doable. So now I always remind myself: just write a little bit today, and a little bit tomorrow, and the day after that. It's easy. Take an hour out of your daily routine, when it's easier for you, and just write as many words as you can. It's really easier than you think."

Balancing your personal life and your writing life can be tricky, especially if you work from home. Suzanne Ruthven puts her writing first. "Everything goes by the wayside when I'm on a writing roll! I tend to work better in the mornings, so once the cottage is tidy and the dogs breakfasted, I get down to work until they get their afternoon meal. If there's nothing interesting on TV, I'll work late into the evening. If there's no pressure to meet a deadline, I'll get the emails out of the way in the morning, and then half an hour or two at the computer during the afternoon."

A M Dunnewin has a different way of balancing her personal

and writing life by combining them. "I balance the two by keeping them together. Whether I'm at work or with friends, I always have that glimpse of an idea or character that I keep to myself until I can get them on paper. Sometimes I carry a notebook around with me, but usually I just contemplate the idea so much that it's stuck in my head even long after I've written it down."

Dealing with Deadlines

If you are happily balanced, maintain a schedule and have a routine to your writing day, then you probably build in your deadlines. When writing a book for instance you might have a six month to a year deadline and it's like a medium term goal, you do a bit every day but it can gather momentum towards the end and leave you racing to meet it. I try to plan my books by giving them weekly deadlines and to me, that's a chapter a week. I sometimes do less and sometimes do more but I set myself that goal so that I know the book is moving forward and will hit my 3 - 6 months target.

But what happens when a deadline comes out of the blue and you wonder if you'll ever meet it? I often write short articles that I might just get two days to submit. Lots of writers who work for websites especially have short deadlines and they have to fit these smaller pieces of work in with the larger. I tell my clients to always schedule in an hour of designated writing time that is open. This means that if something falls in your lap, you've got that extra bit of time to work it in. You could do it on a daily basis or just have that extra hour a week if you are pushed for time, but that way if you are asked for an interview or article, you have that little bit of freedom within your schedule to play with.

Maintaining Momentum

One of the issues that clients often talk to me about is that they lose momentum half way through a story or novel they are writing. I congratulate them because I often only get as far as the first chapter before I've given it up. I've actually just done it again, written a first chapter then after doing some research realised I've got the setting all wrong and scrapped it. This time however I'm not going to give up entirely. I'm going to change the setting, adjust the story and start again.

Especially in fiction writing, some stories are meant to be short whilst others have the elements that could fill a novel. I know some writers are happiest just letting words freeflow and they do not like over-planning their writing but so many other writers will lose momentum if they don't. I'm one of them. If I don't know what is coming up, even vaguely, in each chapter, I'll stall and when that happens it's a short walk to the delete button.

To maintain momentum, especially over a large piece of work, take some time out to think it through and plan for each stage. Break it down into a plot plan, chapter list or timeline and give yourself a place to go when your momentum flags. Like the chunking down technique we previously looked at to make goals more manageable, if you chunk down what you are working on into stages and flesh out those stages, you will never get stuck. You'll know what's coming up next and where your writing is going so your momentum won't have a chance to stall.

Supporting Yourself

Balancing your writing life, juggling the different projects you have underway and just keeping it all running smoothly can take its toil. We're not superhuman although we might like to be. Supporting yourself as a writer is something to build into your writing day and writing life.

There are many ways to support yourself and I'll look at some of them in more depth in chapter six. Techniques like deep breathing, meditation and visualisation can help. Going for a run, walking the dog, or sticking on a fitness DVD can energise you and keep you fit and out of danger of the dreaded writer's bum.

Writers are sitters so we need to exercise, learn stretches, release the tension in our arms and shoulders and look after our backs. We need to learn ways of supporting ourselves physically as well as mentally. Can you build in a physical release into your writing day or week? I go for a daily dog walk but I know other writers that go for a swim, head to the gym for an hour or take time out of their busy day to attend a local keep-fit class.

As well as getting you off of your chair, an amount of daily exercise can invigorate your writing; giving you time to work out ideas, plan the next stage of your writing or imagine your latest characters and their development. Exercise helps the mind to process thoughts and will give you a boost of serotonin – the feel-good hormone – so you'll feel ready to get those words down when you are back at your desk.

Making Others Understand Your Calling

When I was managing a community centre, I had an open door policy. That meant staff could come in and out to me with their queries all day long. Now I am writing, my family seem to think I have the same policy at home. I prop the door open now because otherwise it would be swinging off its hinges every five minutes but there are times when I just cannot take interruptions. I admit I have been known to scream 'Leave me alone!' on occasion.

Unless you have an ivory tower in which to write, you will always have interruptions but it might help to make others in your family understand your calling. Until my boys saw my printed books, they just thought I sat at the computer all day! Talk to your family about what you are working on even if it's not their cup of tea. It's not just about the writing project you are working on; it's about what it means to you.

As writers we often have our heads buried in a book, our eyes focused on the computer or on a notepad and our thoughts somewhere in the land of imagination. It can seem like we are ignoring our nearest and dearest. Writing is a solitary experience and unfortunately they can't be of help (unless you have a partner who is excellent at editing or research!). Talking about what you are working on and why it is important to you can help them to understand why you need your space and what you are hoping to achieve.

Working from home can also pose a problem with friends and family who think you have the time for them just because you are there. It can help to explain that although you are at home you keep working hours and that you won't be available during writing time. The problem with this is that people then think you're making up an excuse not to spend time with them. I always say I'm unavailable in the week but I can meet for coffee or lunch at the weekend. Once friends and family know you are passionate about your work, they'll hopefully respect your focus on writing and if not, unplug the phone, don't answer the door and on no account, use social networking sites that show you are online!

Communication and Making Contacts

It can help to include communication with the outside world as part of your writing day. Even if you don't feel like chatting or it will take up too much of your time, you need to be making contacts. I've noticed that many writers I talk to start their day by checking their emails. They might also update Facebook statuses, use LinkedIn and send a tweet. It helps to do this all in one go and then check in later in the day for replies and to send new messages. The Internet really has become a way in which writers can talk to each other across the globe without the cost or even the hassle of leaving the room (or your pyjamas!).

In my book, *The Writer's Internet*, I talk at length about how writers can utilise the World Wide Web for their own benefit. It really can add to your writing and support you as a communications and networking tool. Take this book for instance that includes quotes from writers that live in Italy, Ireland, the UK, the US – I wouldn't have been able to make contact and receive such quick replies without the use of the Internet. And I've met some amazing writers this way.

Opening yourself up to new ways of communication can help to support your writing life. You'll have a merry band of like-minded people who you can call on for help and advice, tell you of new writing opportunities and be there to share your successes and commiserate with rejections. Some people are wary of networking on the Internet but if you don't give out any personal details like your date of birth or where you live, there shouldn't be a problem. I personally like LinkedIn because your contacts are on a purely professional basis. You can link with other writers, editors, authors and people working in the publishing industry; people you know that you will have something in common with and you can see their credentials in their profile so you know who you are really talking to.

Embracing the Marketplace

Part of any writer's life is to keep an eye on where their work could sell but also to keep an eye on any new opportunities that might present themselves. Again the Internet is a great way of looking for what publishers want, checking out submission details and things like competition and bursary announcements. You probably already check writing magazines and websites but what about seeing what else is out there, that you might be interested in doing and could possibly add to your future goals?

To fully embrace the marketplace, you need to go back to your goals and think where you should be looking and who you should be contacting, even if it's only to keep a check on website updates, read pertinent blogs or sign-up for newsletters. You probably already do this for the main area that your writing covers but what about those other ideas you have that are lurking in there? Say you have the idea for a romance, a historical work, fantasy or sci-fi – do you look at the marketplace for those different types of writing?

We writers often have small inklings of trying out a new genre – something completely different to what we usually write but something that we want to try, just to give it a go and see where it takes us. If this sounds like you, spend some time on finding out what the marketplace is like for this new genre and the next chapter – Crossing Genres – will help you to make the transition to new areas of writing.

Chapter 5

Crossing Genres

Some writers live their life's writing in one vein or one genre. When they achieve success, they continue to cash in on it by producing more and more of the same. There's nothing wrong with that but I have found that more and more writers are diversifying across genres and across different types of writing, from screenwriting to journalism to fiction and blogging and so on. So what do you do if you want to make a change?

Fiction v. Non-fiction

Who says you can't write both? I'm mainly a non-fiction writer but I do love to dabble with fiction and have a few ebooks to my name. I remember starting out writing short stories but the money was in article writing so I stuck with that for years. Talking to other writers I've found that sometimes the decision of what to write is taken out of their hands by opportunity. You might like to write fantasy or historical fiction, romances or mysteries but when you're asked to write a column, send in articles to a weekly magazine or produce copy, you don't say no and you begin to diversify.

Neil McArdle, author and writer, manages to balance both fiction and non-fiction. "When I'm on my game, I'll get a good two or three hours of solid work done, but that might only come in the evening after I've frittered a lot of time doing other stuff. If I'm doing a journalism piece, I'll be out of the house in the day talking to someone. I can churn out a non-fiction story relatively quickly, which is a huge advantage. Fiction comes far slower, and it tends to get written at night, usually quite late. I'm working on a novella at the moment, and some nights I'm happy if I get 400 words. I read somewhere that you shouldn't move on from a scene until it's finished, and I think that's good advice. I have a little room in the house with my ancient computer. My back is to the window. On the wall in front of me are my bills. It's a good motivator."

Changing Direction

Whenever your writing stalls or you're fed up with receiving another rejection, you could think about changing direction. Change can appear scary, difficult or worrying – if you let it, but change is positive. Changing to other genres or embracing new forms of writing can open you up to a whole new world.

Change is forward motion. It's a process of making a decision and taking action to move you along a new path. When you decide to make a change in your writing career, it can give you new-found pleasure in your creativity, a fresh glow of achievement and as your new writing direction becomes recognised so your confidence and self-esteem will be boosted. With a change in direction, you will be free to include other writing genres in your life and achieve goals that you never thought were possible.

Change doesn't have to be drastic. You don't have to give up fiction for non-fiction or stop writing poetry so that you can write stage plays. But you can take little steps towards new horizons by adding in new projects, however small, to your writing routine.

Believing in New Projects

New projects require your commitment and belief. If you don't believe in yourself as a writer and a writer capable of new things, then you can't expect anyone to read them. If you're sitting there thinking I'll give this a go but your heart's not in it, it will show in your writing whatever genre that may be.

When we choose to change genres, we face a challenge. It can cause us to fear change. We might not want to experience a loss of something that we have worked on for so long but if we look at it as not losing but leaving something behind, through our own choice, it makes the experience much more positive. And sometimes you do have to let things go.

I know that perseverance is key for writers. Publication doesn't happen overnight for most of us and it takes years of hard work before our writing is recognised, but sometimes it is time to say this isn't working for me and I need to change to a new genre. I have had many clients come to me who think that they are fiction writers. I'm not sure why but in my experience, when people think of writing they think of fiction first. I've known people to struggle for years and years to have their short stories or novel published but maybe, just maybe, that isn't what they were meant to write.

When you look at writing as an industry and think of all the other types of writing that are out there, it might just be one of those that will welcome a struggling writer with open arms. What about business writing, copywriting, textbook writing, web, technical, how-to, advert and academic writing, screen-writing, radio play writing, speech writing – phew! The list goes on and it is so varied. There is so much on offer in the world of writing that to stay fixed on one type does you no favours. Sure, if you are making millions by writing in one genre and the work just keeps coming then you have made it but if you are strug-gling, need something to change in your writing life and are fed up with not getting anywhere then it could be time to change direction and start believing in a new project.

Anna McPartlin, author of several novels including No Way to Say Goodbye and The Truth Will Out has this to say, "Storytelling is simply the ability to write a good yarn so the only obstacle to transitioning between fiction or non-fiction, screen-writing or novels, adults' or kids' stories is a good idea and passion for the genre. I would never write horror no matter how popular because horror bores me, the same can be said of The 50 Shades phenomenon, titillation may be the new money maker but it doesn't thrill me at all. I'm passionate about comedy, drama and big characters, they are the ingredients in all my goo and ultimately the characters and story decide the genre not the writer.

So my one and only tip is that if you love what you do, if you are confident in your story and you want to venture into a new genre just do it, the worst that can happen is that others won't be as passionate about that story or your way of telling it but so what? You'll enjoy it, you'll learn from it and you'll tell the stories you want to tell the way you want to tell them. In doing that, you will find your way."

Managing Transitions

Negative self-talk can dissuade writers from even taking those first steps into trying something new. We say things like 'I've never had something published like that before so I won't bother trying' or 'What if nobody likes my fiction writing?' or 'Maybe I'm just meant to be a (insert your current genre here) writer' and yet again we talk ourselves out of something that could really energise us and invigorate our writing.

Amanda J Evans, author of *From Those Death Left Behind,* says, "Negative thoughts always creep in and like most writers I do have a tendency to compare my work to others. I sometimes feel that my work isn't good enough but I have a solid network of friends, family and clients who are always quick to point out the quality of my work. Negative thoughts mainly affect my personal writing and this includes fear of failure and of not being good enough. My way of combating this is to make a list of my accomplishments at the end of each day. If I get just one blog post completed or three pages of my novel, it is an accomplishment and I make note of it. At the end of the week I read back and see all the things I have accomplished. This helps to ward off negative thoughts. Pushing through the negative thoughts is another thing I enjoy along with reading positive affirmations and quotes. I use the 'tell my story' technique and visualisations too. I think negative thoughts are something that will always lurk but learning how to handle and overcome them is the key and I feel that I have discovered how to allow myself to do just this."

One way to overcome these thoughts, especially when starting a new project, is to use balancing statements. When you catch yourself saying negative thoughts, jot them down and then rewrite them in a more positive, realistic way. So saying 'I've never had something published like that before so I won't bother trying' can turn into 'I've never had something published like that so this is a great opportunity for me to show a new side to my skills'. Start a new direction with positive thoughts about the outcome and give yourself the freedom to make a change.

Is It Worth It?

You might be wondering whether you should even bother crossing genres especially if you are well within your comfort zone with your main writing genre. But nothing ventured, nothing gained, as the saying goes and at some point an idea will come to you that doesn't sit in that zone and makes you want to try something new.

Here's an exercise you can do to rate these new ideas that are buzzing around your head and see whether they are worth your time and energy. Set up a spreadsheet or table with seven columns and as many rows as you have ideas. Then add in your column headings:

1 Your idea
2 How easy it will be to do
3 Cost – are there research costs involved?
4 The impact on yourself – if this idea was successful, how good would that make you feel?
5 The impact on your family – will it give you more time

with them? Less?

6   Overall rating

7   Best idea

Mark 2, 3, 4, and 5 with a score between 1-10, one being the more negative, 10 being the more positive, then add them all together to give each idea its overall rating in column number six. Once you have done this for each idea, tick against the top three highest scoring ideas. What have you got to lose by trying these out? If they make you happy and fulfilled, don't have an adverse affect on your family, and are easy and cost-effective to do then the change to that new genre could be well worth your while pursuing.

Accomplishing Change

One way of working towards a new genre is to use a technique used by NLP practitioners called modelling. Modelling is a way of looking at someone who we admire or wish to learn from and, in seeing how they accomplish their successes; we can learn how to achieve our own. If you know another writer who has been successful in a genre you are considering trying, then talk to them, find out how they got their big break or their foot in the door and what they attribute their achievements to. If you can't find a writer you know then look online in forums and chat rooms to see what those genre writers are talking about. Look at their work and where it was published. Is there an opportunity there for you?

Read interviews they've given, watch TV shows they've appeared on and see if you can find out more about them through their website or blog. I'm not advocating that you copy them – plagiarism is a sin! – just assess why they are successful in their particular area of writing so that you can pick up tips, advice and knowledge to help you with a change in your own skills.

Use the knowledge that you gain to set yourself new projects.

Start by planning small ways in which you can embrace a new genre or new method of writing. Could you start reading more in that genre? Join an organisation with like-minded writers? Enter a competition or get professional feedback on a new piece of work?

Change doesn't come overnight. It's a gradual process that takes time. You might really want to try something new but you still have to pay the bills through your regular writing so how about just building in the time to start working in a new direction. Remember I said before about having a spare hour pencilled into your writing schedule? You could start by using that to cross genres and accomplish change in your writing life.

A Positive Story

Freelance journalist and writer, Joe Griffin, took the plunge and made a change. Here's his story.

"I initially wanted to be a full-time film critic and I worked towards that for a number of years; I've written for numerous papers and magazines both in Ireland and the UK on the subject. I love it, and still love writing about it, but eventually I learned that it just wasn't feasible for me to make a living out of it. I'd initially started branching out to other interests like music, theatre, TV and comedy, and then expanded to write about technology, lifestyle, news and especially videogames. In all that time I'd been dabbling in writing fiction, intermittently, as a hobby. Writing fiction is an entirely different discipline and challenge – in many ways more difficult than journalism, but ultimately more gratifying. Now I'd classify myself as a freelance journalist and writer.

Changing direction is essential not only for making a living as a journalist and writer, but also in maintaining your interest in writing. Even something as phenomenally exciting as film criticism can get repetitive when you've watched one Adam Sandler film too many: You have no idea how many bad films there are until you start reviewing them one by one!

LIFE COACHING FOR WRITERS

It's important to nurture your different interests, even if you're only writing about one subject. For example, in film criticism, having a decent knowledge of history would help you better interpret and appreciate a historical drama. But my transition was quite organic; a play or film set in another country might get you interested in that country's politics; a music documentary might introduce you to a new band or genre you hadn't heard.

Once you've made any start in writing about one particular subject, you'll find that editors are slightly more open to using your copy on other subjects, and you'll find it easier to make contact with different editors within the same outlets (be it a newspaper or publishing house). Sometimes you have to continue writing about the old subject while you're getting started in the new, and that's fine too.

I didn't overanalyse new writing projects, which I think helped enormously. If you think too long about doing something, you'll find reasons not to do it. For many stories you don't have to be an expert in something to write about it, but you have to know how to find the people to talk to about it, how to get the most out of them and how to interpret and express the information you've gathered.

And people often underestimate the depth of knowledge and skill they've accumulated in their lives; whether they've been working in a particular field, studied it, or it's just a hobby or interest they're passionate about."

Other Ways to Support Yourself Financially as a Writer

What else can writers do to support themselves when they are writing? Great, you might have a book contract but the advance may be small and the royalties aren't pouring in it, so what do you do? Many writers continue to have a job outside of their writing careers to pay the bills but other writers embrace the wider world of writing and this can lead them to new and fresh genre pastures.

I know writers who are also editors, copyeditors, publicists and cover designers. I also know writers who are lecturers, college teachers and distance learning tutors. Then there's the brave ones who like getting out there and who run their own courses, deliver workshops and are paid to give talks and attend conferences.

A lot of extra work is found through the Internet; blogging, writing articles, reviews, copywriting and providing web content. And then there's selling yourself and your own skills by coaching or being a consultant and marketing yourself to beginner writers as a guide and professional expert.

What else could you do? Have a look around for new opportunities, check in with contacts so see if they know of any openings and be open to what changes you could add into your writing life that will support you financially.

Giving up the Day Job

If you can make a living from your writing or if you can diversify enough to bring home the bacon or veggieburgers, you may get to the point where you can give up your day job.

For Marilynn Hughes it was a gradual process, "It slowly morphed to where I could no longer do anything else. In the beginning, I often worked four or so part-time jobs to help support the writing. Suddenly, I started noticing more money was coming in from the writing and my energies were more fruitful there, so when my last contract to teach a class expired, I stopped doing anything else."

Nik Morton says "I retired early and moved to Spain and immediately saw my output increase. However, I've also been an editor for other publishers, so a portion of my working day is allocated to them."

Suzanne Ruthven took a gamble that worked when she made the change to starting her own magazine. "I'd been working full-time as a writer since 1987 when I made the decision to go freelance and start 'Quartos' my first creative writing magazine. My years as an international conference organiser meant that I could finance my gamble. Luckily, it paid off."

Deborah Durbin waited for the right time to give up the day job. "I only started writing for a living when my second daughter, who is now 16, was born because I wanted a job where I could work mostly from home. Because writing is my full-time occupation I have to make it work, so that's good motivation to get those fingers on the keyboard!"

Amanda J Evans also became a mum and wanted to work from home. "For ten years I worked in the local hospital. In 2004, I discovered that you could get paid to write. It was like a dream come true and I began researching. I signed up for a website called Elance and everything started from there. I began writing for clients and really enjoyed it. Getting paid for it was an even bigger bonus. By the time I was expecting my second child in 2006, I was making two salaries and the decision to become a stay at home mom was easy. Since then I have narrowed my focus and created a solid routine. I have built a client list and also write for myself. My success came from setting goals and having clear direction for what I wanted to achieve. I wanted to be able to maintain my lifestyle whilst still being able to be at home with my children. This is exactly what I have achieved."

Crossing genres and embracing change in your writing career can lead to enough work so that you too will be able to concentrate on your writing full time. Are there any changes you'd like to make starting now?

Chapter 6

Looking after Yourself

Everyone is guilty of not looking after themselves at times. We put everything else first – home, family, friends, work – before we think to mind ourselves. Writers need to look after themselves especially when they are working in a solitary environment with not much support or companionship. Many of us like this solitude and it makes us appreciate our friends and family more when we catch up with them but it can also lead to too much introspection and a build up of stress.

Now Relax

It's important for us writers to find ways to relax that don't always involve copious amounts of wine and smoking twenty cigarettes! Everyone needs their vices but there are much healthier options.

Niall McArdle has found that music is a great relaxant. "I got rid of cable and I don't have the internet, so I've been able to remove two huge distractions. I drink a lot of coffee and listen to a lot of music. I listen to anything and everything, but I tend to listen to a lot of the same stuff over and over and over. I'll play the same CD six times in a row because I don't want to get too distracted from what I'm writing. The music is there in the background, but it becomes like white noise. It does slip into the subconscious, though. I listened to a Leonard Cohen album ten times in a row every night for two weeks. It's the one with "The Story of Isaac." It's not a coincidence that the story I was working on at the time ended up riffing on the story of Abraham and Isaac."

Meadhbh Boyd says "Read everything – Heat magazine, novels, newspapers, blogs, tweets, other social media.

Regardless of the medium, feed your mind with all styles of expression. Experience the world. It is the world that inspires most of us to write, our experiences of being in the world. If you have writer's block, it's probably down to the fact that you have not been good to yourself, you have not been to a gallery, seen a film, had a manicure, chatted with a friend. Get out of the bubble."

Meadhbh makes an important point that as writers we live too much in our own bubbles and that taking time out to look after ourselves will ultimately benefit our writing.

Stress Management Techniques

Writers are stressed by so many things; deadlines looming, another rejection, the need to be published, the stack of bills that mount up between writing projects as well as everyday stresses and strains. A client recently said to me that although they loved writing and making a career from their work, it was probably the most unstable career they had ever had from never knowing when the next payment is going to come in to wondering if they will ever really make enough to live on.

There are lots of ways in which you can reduce the stress that a writing life brings and I'm going to touch on a few of those here but one of the most important factors in dealing with stress is to recognise it when you are experiencing it. Stress can often rear its head through physical symptoms; headaches, mood swings, stomach aches, irritability, back pain, etc. and we put it down to not feeling well rather than admitting that we have a lot going on and we feel stressed.

Body awareness is extremely important in stress management. Whenever we feel stressed, we tense our bodies even without realising it. Our body reacts first and our minds only register it afterwards. If at all. People under constant stress become so used to it that they don't feel the damage it is doing to their bodies.

I worked in a very stressful job for many years and thought

that I was on top of it all. I had massages for tension, carried around remedies for headaches and put my constantly churning stomach down to IBS. It wasn't until I had surgery and everything had to stop while I recovered that I realised how much stress I had been carrying around on my shoulders and once I recognised it, I wanted to let it go. So I took a course in stress management and learnt techniques to help myself and to pass on to my clients.

One of the easiest and most calming relaxation techniques to use is that of deep breathing. It's a technique that you can use when you are on the go to instantly calm your nerves. Breathing deeply re-oxygenates your body. When we are stressed, angry or frustrated, our breath is shallow and comes in short, sharp bursts. By slowing our breathing and allowing more air to enter our bodies, we start to calm. To try this, breathe in through your nose for the count of four, really filling your lungs, and then breathe out through your mouth with a count of four. Do this several times until you feel its calming effect. If you can shut yourself away somewhere quiet or get outside to somewhere peaceful and calming, it will also help.

There are many relaxation techniques you can try but one particularly good one is all body relaxation. This is good for unwinding after a long day and can be done in the bath or when you are in bed to help you drift off to sleep. The idea is to flex and stretch each part of your body and then tell it to relax. So start with your toes, scrunch them up and let them go, move your ankles and then let them relax, go up to your calves, your knees and so on until you get to your head, moving and then relaxing each body part. You can do this a couple of times and use the deep breathing technique as well until all your body feels rested.

Visualisation and meditation are two other popular relaxation techniques. Meditation can be used to help clear your mind of negative thoughts and to relax your body. Some people like to listen to soothing sounds while they meditate but others like complete silence. Try sitting in a quiet room, concentrate on your breathing and clear your mind. If you have difficulty stopping your thoughts whirling you can either use a mantra or concentrate on a visualisation. Mantras are sayings that you repeat over and over again like 'I am calm' or 'I am relaxed'. Try saying words like calm, peace, relax and rest to focus your thoughts. You can also use visualisation to help you de-stress. Think of places that mean serenity and calmness to you like a beautiful garden, a beach, or a forest and imagine that you are there just walking in nature and feeling safe, secure and at peace. These positive calming thoughts will help you to relax and unwind from your writing life and the stresses it brings.

Affirmations and Check-ins

I love the description of affirmation on Wikipedia. It says 'a declaration that something is true'. No disputing that, is there? I have a daily affirmation sent to my inbox each morning and I then try to see that from a writer's perspective or how it relates to my writing self as well as the holistic me. In fact there are lots of websites that will give you mantras, affirmations and ways to check-in with yourself that you can have delivered regularly or you can log onto them on a daily basis if you need some food for thought and some positive reinforcement.

Check-ins are times when you seriously say hello me, how are you doing? And you spend a half hour, an hour, just reviewing how you feel and how you are doing. It's like reviewing your goals but from a more emotional point of view. Instead of the business side of getting things done and checking the progress you are making, it's looking at all those writing projects and saying how do I feel about this? I must admit that I do a check-in with a glass of wine in hand on a night when my house is quiet and everyone's out. I love sitting with my lists and seeing what I've achieved and what hasn't worked so well as a sort of personal review. This can be a time when I come up with new ideas or cross off ones that I haven't managed to get round to and I can let go but what it really does is ground me in a sense of self and the knowledge of where I am with my writing.

One of my clients had a bad experience with a publisher. When her book was published, she was given the impression it would be a best-seller and her career would be taking off. She gave up her day job and started writing her next book. But her first book wasn't marketed very well and as a result, the sales were poor. She was absolutely devastated and it completely undermined her belief in herself as a writer. I asked her to just try daily affirmations as a way of building her confidence again and to give her positive thoughts as she began her day every morning. She also did a check-in and looked at how this experience had hurt her and left her feeling vulnerable. She realised she would have to work through her negative experience before she felt like she could trust a publisher again but she saw that she could – her writing self was still there – it just needed extra care and attention and a daily affirmation was a start to regaining her former confidence.

Daily Gratitudes

Here's something that I do every night before I go to sleep and it's especially useful on those down days when you don't feel so good about yourself or your writing. You can do it at any time of the day but thinking about what you are grateful for last thing at night can set you up for a good night's sleep and give you a positive start to the next morning.

You basically list five things that you are grateful for. So last night I was grateful for having the opportunity to deliver a talk on life-writing, for seeing my third non-fiction book go into production, for having a healthy and happy family, for enjoying an evening cuddle with my dog and for getting some research done for a fiction novel. Once you start listing what you are grateful for you actually end up with a lot more than five things and it's just a reminder of the good things in life, the friends and family you share your time with, the opportunities that come your way and it's a pat on the back for the things you have achieved. Even on days when you don't get much writing done, there's lots to be grateful for and reminding yourself of this can boost your mood.

Get Exercising

I mentioned exercise in chapter four as a way of supporting your writing self and giving yourself time to think and it's also a great way to boost your mood.

Deborah Durbin says, "I have a fear of developing writer's bum, so I make sure I go to the gym three times a week. I also specialise in health and wellbeing, so I have a good idea of how to keep in tip-top shape."

Exercise is the ultimate stress relief not only because it physically takes you away from stressful situations but because it rids your body of toxins, releases those feel-good endorphins into your bloodstream, strengthens your muscles and relieves tension and clears your mind so that you can think through your emotions and clarify what your goals and aims are.

But it's something we often talk ourselves out of with excuses like it's too cold to go for a walk, gym membership is too expensive and it's just too boring. The trick is to find some form of exercise that you like doing. There must be something!

And your body needs it. As writers we spend so much time sitting, we hunch our shoulders over a keyboard, bend our necks whilst reading and live a fairly sedentary life unless we add in ways to exercise. I'm sure you've read articles about small ways in which to become fitter like walking to work instead of catching the bus or climbing the stairs instead of taking a lift. If you look at your daily routine, is there some way in which you can add exercise into it – even if it's just 10 minutes? Or can you add in a weekly exercise like joining a class or going for a swim? Your body and your stress levels will start to benefit from the minute you start to increase your physical activity and this in turn will aid your writing.

Dealing with Limiting Beliefs

I've talked about beliefs several times so far and you may be thinking 'enough with the beliefs' by now! But there's just one more thing...

We talked about change in the last chapter and although our beliefs begin forming from the minute we are born, they can also be changed at any time during our lives. Dealing with beliefs that limit our lives and cause us stress is part of looking after ourselves. Just take a moment to see what you say to yourself that is actually a limiting belief. They are often phrased as *shoulds*, *musts* and *oughts* and include a *but* in there somewhere. As in I must be a better writer but I don't think I can be or I should make more time for my writing but I don't think that I can. Check out your self-talk for any limiting beliefs and like the exercise on turning negative thoughts into more positive ones, omit these from your thinking and replace them with open statements like 'I am the best writer' or 'I can cross genres' and leave out the buts!

How to Take Care of Your Writing Self

I wondered how other writers look after their selves and what makes them feel good about their writing so I asked some writing friends for their thoughts on how they look after their selves. Here are some of their stories.

Joe Griffin told me, "At the risk of sounding obvious, nothing beats reading. When not writing, I try – not always successfully – to make time to read, and everything helps in its own way. Non-fiction could make your fiction writing more believable: Reading about a war zone, for example, would be of use to a horror writer; reading a good autobiography would help you develop character; a magazine article might have an elegant turn of phrase or a viewpoint you disagree with; and of course, reading authors you admire (fiction or non-fiction) will develop your craft. Even taking in other forms of art and storytelling has – I believe – helped me. From films to TV to documentaries to videogames to art to theatre to music, genius comes in many forms."

Amanda J Evans told me, "My writing self is the real me and the force that drives me forward. Whenever client work gets too much or becomes boring I find that a break and a little perspective really helps. Taking walks and playing with my children really helps as does some quiet time. I enjoy meditating which really helps with story ideas and to boost my creativity. I try to balance my client work with my personal writing. I also love learning and reading and enjoy brain stimulation. Free writing is another little exercise that I enjoy. For this I normally involve my children and we have some fun picking a word and then making up a story about it."

Melinda Feeney has a great suggestion, "I give myself permission to be a child and imagine things. I'm not sure who decided adults need to be so serious all the time." And A M Dunnewin enjoys, "Daydreaming, music, and lots and lots of reading. Sometimes I have to get out of my own head so I don't over think my own story."

Avoiding Burnout

Burnout can occur when your stress levels reach their peak. Things like taking on too much work, having too many deadlines to meet, and getting too many rejections can make you feel like you are never getting anywhere with your writing. Burnout is the ultimate writer's block where you just can't get anything done because you can't see a clear path ahead. Niall McArdle comments, "I mean proper writer's block: not the kind that people imagine (pacing the room searching for the perfect word); the real awful kind, the kind of writer's block where you haven't written anything for months and you're sitting in your pyjamas at two in the afternoon watching game shows."

On a TV quiz show I watched (you don't have to have writer's block to suffer from this affliction!), the contestant froze mid-answer and try as she might she just could not pick up the train of her thoughts. That's what burnout is like, when everything rushes past you but you can't seem to stop and concentrate on anything and if you don't look after yourself, burnout can occur.

You can avoid ever getting into this state by organising, planning, goal setting and giving yourself time to accomplish what you want to achieve. Some writers especially at the beginning of their careers push themselves to work and work, saying yes to every request and trying their hardest to do it all. But we aren't wonder men and women; we can't possibly do everything and not suffer for it at some point. And the best way to avoid burnout is to learn to say no even if it means losing a commission, even if it means turning down an opportunity. If you feel like you are heading for burnout, clear your diary, take time out and cross off some of the things on your to-do list. They can wait.

Chapter 7

Success and Rejection

Writing must be one of the hardest careers to crack and it can take years of successes and rejections before any writer feels like they have made it. But what about celebrating those small successes that you have along the way? Do you take time out to pat yourself on the back and congratulate your creative self on what you achieve? We also know that rejection is a part of the publishing process and it happens to every writer however great they are. By thinking of a negative response as feedback instead of failure, we can learn to feel more positive about the process and move on with our writing careers.

You Can Do It – and You Have Done!

What constitutes a success? When we first start writing for publication, it's just having something in print, something we have written that is accepted by an editor or publisher. It takes a new physical form and turns into a different format like that of a magazine article, book or online story. Once we're through that hurdle, we can say we are truly writers and then we seem to get tough on ourselves. I know writers that churn out hundreds of articles but don't stop to think of that achievement because it isn't their ultimate goal. Their articles and short stories pay the bills and they are a means to an end, adding to a portfolio and creating an online or magazine presence, but they aren't truly celebrated.

If this sounds like you, just remember there are loads of beginner writers out there who still haven't had anything published. What you do is actually amazing, no matter whether it makes you feel successful or not. It doesn't matter how big or small the success is – what matters is that you have achieved a goal. Can you remember what it was like, right at the start of your writing career, to feel so desperate to have something published or to really want your first book contract and you'd do anything to get it? When we want something really badly, it can seem like it takes forever for it to come to us but once we have had some of our work published, we start to ignore the smaller successes because we've had them before.

My point is success can be big and yes, we've all got dreams of what that looks like to us, but success can also be small and it is in every article you have published, every story of yours that ends up in print, every competition you win, every interview you give – it's in all the small things that build us up to be a successful writer.

Celebrating Success

How often do you actually celebrate your successes? We rarely take time to acknowledge all the successes we've had. In chapter six, I talked about having daily gratitudes which you can use to be grateful for the successes that come your way but what about actually celebrating all the times when you have achieved something positive in your writing career?

If it was your wedding anniversary, a partner's birthday or a child's engagement, you might have a party to celebrate or you might mark the occasion in some way like going for a meal, having a night on the tiles or celebrating at home with a bottle of the finest wine, but how often do you say it's been a year since I started writing professionally and I'm going to celebrate that or I've just published my third, fourth, fifth book and I think I'm due a party?

Some of us find it hard to congratulate ourselves so here are a few tips from other writers.

For Amanda J Evans, celebrating success is a family affair, "Success is celebrated with all my family. When I published *Messages From The Angelic Realms* last year, a group of my friends got together and created a special night where I could launch my book and give a talk. It was a wonderful night and all my family and friends were there to support me. My husband is great and loves to celebrate even the smallest successes. He will surprise me with dinner or a nice treat. My children, especially my daughter, like to make me little cards and write me notes that say congratulations. I celebrate by writing myself little letters every time I accomplish one of my goals. It is a little like inner child work where I give myself praise and recognition for what I have accomplished."

Meadhbh Boyd also finds relationships important. She suggests, "Some decent coffee and yummy cake, or buy a nice bottle of wine, curl up and watch a film with someone you love, whether it's a girlfriend, boyfriend or relative. You should share the good times when they happen. "

Lawrence Wray thinks you should treat yourself, "Buy something expensive that you and only you really appreciate. For me it's pens and watches, but whatever you desire as a reward works. Doesn't have to be a million bucks, just something that takes your fancy, but only when you actually have that success."

Nik Morton already has a bottle chilling. "Open a bottle of Cava. And then continue work on the next project, which I'll already have begun even before the last one is sent out."

The next time you have an article published, receive a commission or a contract, or have any writing success, celebrate your creativity and congratulate yourself for all the work you've done. It'll give you a boost and help you to maintain momentum, pushing you forward to achieve your next goal.

Congratulating Your Creative Self

In NLP, success isn't just about the outcome of your goals and your achievements; it's about the process that you took to get there. When you achieve success, you take a certain route and you learn what works on the way. Each route is peppered with the steps you took to achieve that success so your creative self has mastered stages that you can utilise again. When starting a new writing project, it can help to analyse what you did at each stage so that you can copy those elements of success and use them again to your advantage. I know in the world of writing, success is often up to fate, luck or the opportunities that present themselves but if you have achieved success just once, you have learnt a pattern that can be repeated and once you know this, rejection cannot harm you!

Think of ways in which you can say thank you to yourself and congratulate your creative self on taking those steps to success. Deborah Durbin celebrates in different ways, "It all depends on how big the success is. If I get a new commission for a magazine or newspaper feature, I take my daughters out for lunch. If I get a new book commission, I go shopping – usually for another diamond ring!"

Joe Griffin also does things differently depending on the scale of the success, "This sounds childish, but when I first got published in The Guardian the first thing I did was ring my mother! Otherwise I celebrate in big ways (going out for dinner and then dancing like a lunatic) or small ways (sticking a Prince song on YouTube and dancing). I guess I like dancing!"

The next time something works well for you, congratulate your creative self in a creative way. Dance around the room like Joe, sing your heart out or paint a picture full of bright, vivid colours. Immerse yourself in your creativity and let yourself feel really, really great!

Fear of Success

Some writers fear success. Talking generally, we work in a vacuum, in our own little bubbles, shut away from the world as we work on our masterpieces. With success comes taking a step out into the world and interacting with people who might buy our books, see our plays and films or come to our book signings. It can be a shock to any writer to move into that world when they have been so used to spending their days alone or in solitude albeit with a computer for company.

You don't have to step outside into the wider world of success and self-promotion – you can stay forever in your bubble if you really want to but most publishers nowadays want their writers to promote their own work and there are so many opportunities to get out there and make a name for yourself, that it's an opportunity wasted if you don't. Ultimately you write because you want your work to be read so talking to your readers is only going to bring you more sales.

Take each step towards success as a challenge and prepare for it. Say you are asked to give a talk to thirty people – what is the worst that can happen? We've talked before about ways to deal with new challenges and our thought processes around them are the key. Think positively and be open to the other elements of a writing life. And if like me, nerves sometimes get the better of you, have a calming kit at the ready. I have lavender oil in my bag for soothing the jitters, Rescue Remedy to calm my nerves and chamomile teabags for relieving tension. What could you have with you to support you when you step out into the wide world and embrace your successes as a writer?

It's not Failure!

Failure is a dirty word in life coaching and NLP because it doesn't exist. There is no such thing as failure only feedback. Every time that you do something that doesn't seem to go too well, it's not failure, you are just receiving feedback, no matter how negative that seems to be.

Most of us have been through the rejection procedure and will know that rejections come in a variety of ways from the standard no thank you to not hearing anything at all to getting some kind of comments and er, feedback!

I wrote a fantasy story at the beginning of my writing career and sent it off to a fantasy magazine who returned my manuscript with 'what's the point?' scrawled across it. It absolutely devastated me – did they mean what's the point of the story? Or what's the point in me ever trying to write again? I'd actually written the story as part of a writing course and I knew that it was legible and made sense (or so my tutor thought). So I sent it out again and this time it was accepted and published. The editor actually said she loved it. That one piece of feedback could have ended my writing career but I learnt from it. It was just one person's point of view and another person, editor or publisher could have a completely different perspective.

One of my clients came to me utterly dejected about her manuscript being returned yet again. She had given up hours of her time and worked part-time so that she could fulfil her dream of writing a book but she couldn't find a publisher. She talked about being a failure. I asked her what she had set out to do. Write a book was her answer. We talked about why she felt that was a failure when she had obviously done what she had hoped to achieve. She had successfully accomplished her goal. The goal was to write a book and, although publishing it was always at the back of her mind, she needed to congratulate herself on what she had done so far. I asked her if any publisher had given her feedback and she did have some comments that she could constructively work on to improve her manuscript. We talked about what she could do next and looked at self-publishing and preparing her manuscript as an e-book as another option.

If you think feedback instead of failure, it opens doors to improvement. Failure is a dead end that leaves you feeling bad and negative about your writing. Feedback is a learning process. So your manuscript is returned, what can you do to make it better? What publisher can you try next? Is there a way of breaking your non-fiction book idea down into a series of articles, serialising your story online in a blog or producing your manuscript as an e-book? With feedback, there are always alternatives and always other options for a writer to try out.

Dealing with Rejection

Rejection makes us generalise. We wail things like 'no publisher will ever publish my book', 'all my writing is rubbish' and 'no one is ever going to read my work'. All of a sudden everyone is against us, nothing is ever going to go right and it's the end of your writing career. We do it to ourselves but in truth, you don't know that no publisher is going to print your book; you cannot say that all your writing is rubbish, especially if you've had other successes, and of course someone will read your work somewhere and at sometime. Watch out for the generalisations you make that put you in a bad mood and don't let rejection get the better of you.

Deborah Durbin has some good advice, "If you're going to be a writer you have to accept that rejection is part and parcel of the job. I've been writing professionally for 16 years now, so it doesn't bother me anymore, but initially I would question what I had done wrong and why an editor didn't like my work. The longer you write the more confident you come across in your pitches and you soon learn how to approach different editors and what works and what doesn't."

Amanda J Evans says, "Rejection is a part of writing and not everyone will like what I write. It took me a long time to understand this but now I look at rejection in a different way. When I receive a rejection, I realise that the person rejecting it is not rejecting me but the writing and that it just isn't a fit for them. For many writers rejection is their worst fear but when you realise that it is not you who is being rejected, it becomes so much easier. Rejection is a part of writing and to even receive a rejection is an acknowledgement that your work was read. The more in-depth the rejection the better your writing actually was. We can all learn to improve our writing and rejection helps us to do just this. Every time I receive a rejection I silently thank the person for their help and for allowing me to improve. I don't see rejection as failure but as a way to grow and learn."

Krystina Kellingley lets herself feel low for only a moment, "I feel dispirited but make myself get back on track and send my work to another place." This is something that many writers do. They just send their work out again. A M Dunnewin says, "I immediately rewrite my proposal, and send it off to someone else. I use to be depressed when I received rejections, but now I just see it as a challenge." Suzanne Ruthven, editor of Compass Books, gives similar advice, "Study the reason for the rejection and then re-jig the article or proposal to send out to another editor or publisher."

Nik Morton says, "It depends on the rejection. If it's constructive, I'll weigh up the comments, they may have foundation. That's rare, these days, though, as editors and publishers are fearful of making comment as they're liable to get Internet abuse from a few unprofessional bad apples. Usually, I find an alternative recipient/market and send it out again."

Yes, rejection hurts and yes, it doesn't give you a positive feeling about your skills as a writer but as you well know by now there are a hundred and one reasons for a rejection and the opposite of that is a hundred and one reasons why something that is rejected by one publisher or editor can be accepted by another. Every writer I spoke to about rejection just got on with their next project or sent out their writing to a new market. The only way to deal with rejection is to ignore it, don't take it to heart and keep writing.

Planning for the Future

Each success brings you closer and closer to your ultimate goal until one day that success is the big one, the thing you've always worked towards, the thing you waited for. When your success is so monumental, you might well celebrate it and bask in all your glory for a few days before you begin to think – er, I did that, so what's next?

At any stage of your writing career, you can stop to appreciate where you are and what you have achieved. If you've gained your goals and made huge achievements, you might start to flounder, wondering what you will do in the future. You can always go back to your goals and try some brainstorming or other exercises to see where you're going next but you can also use a visualisation to get a glimpse of yourself in the future.

As with any visualisation, make sure you are comfortable, warm and in a quiet space before you start. Close your eyes and regulate your breathing by taking deep breaths until you feel a sense of calm.

Imagine you are meeting your future self. You have everything you need; your house is the way you want it, your family are happy and healthy, the car of your dreams is in the garage – all those material things have been achieved and there is nothing in your path except...

You are a writer still and you are living the life you have always wanted. What are you working on? What have been your successes so far? What are you most proud of? What can you show your current self that you have achieved? Follow your future writing self to their writing area – what's on their vision board? What's pinned up on the wall? What books are on the shelf? What appointments are in their diary? Are they going to a premiere of the film they wrote, a play at the theatre, an award winning ceremony? Look around to see what they – you in the future – have achieved and soak in what you still have to do.

Let your mind drift around the possibilities that are still open to you and then return to concentrate on your breathing. When you feel ready, open your eyes and come back to your current self. If you have found new inspiration, ideas or possibilities for your future, write them down in your journal or notebook. More successes are on their way.

Chapter 8

When the Going gets Tough

We all have times in our lives when the going gets tough. The work may not be coming in, the bills are mounting up, our relationship is suffering and family must come first – plus all the things that life throws at us from moving house to combating illness to losing someone we love. Life isn't easy at times and as a writer, you have a key skill at your fingertips to help you through those difficult times.

Getting it Down on Paper

Here's a thought – how often do you write for yourself? I mean really for yourself. You can sit down and write out your feelings, your emotions and all the things that you have pent up inside to ease you through troubled times. You're a writer; you know how to do it! So you can use your writing skills to support yourself and help you to deal with the tough times in life.

There has been a lot of research done lately that looks at writing as a therapeutic medium. Many hospitals and therapy centres encourage their patients and clients to write down the issues they are dealing with to release internal pressure and help them to clarify their thoughts.

You can be your own therapist with some of the activities in this chapter. You won't have to make an appointment or travel miles to a meeting. You can sit in your own comfortable space with pen and paper and create your own counselling session. It's worth a try if only to save on medical bills!

Reframing the Issue

Writing it all down can help you to reframe the issue you are facing. Another NLP technique, this is used for helping you to look at a problem or issue from a different perspective. Is this tough time that you are going through really a way to say goodbye to the old and hello to the new? Are you going through a bad patch so that you can come out of it stronger and wiser? Is this a learning process that no matter how hard it seems at the time will actually liberate you when you get through it?

There are some challenges that we face in life that are truly distressing but reframing the situation can help you to see the light. Reframing your thoughts around a situation gives it a new meaning. So you lost your job and that is tough but is it really an opportunity to write full-time on that project you've always wanted to do?

You can also reframe your challenges visually. It works better for some people if they visualise their situation like a photograph, a snapshot of what they are not happy with. You then mentally create a new photo, a new image that you replace the old one with. Deleting the old photo for a new more positive one can help you to look at an issue in a different way and maybe it's not such an issue after all but an opportunity for change.

Using Diaries

I don't know how you feel about sharing your emotional life with other people. I've written many articles that draw on my own experiences but sometimes you do wonder if you want to bare your soul quite as much. I started out by writing parenting articles and my boys who are now grown up cringe at the sight of them and have told me I'm not allowed to write about them anymore! Sharing your life stories isn't everyone's cup of tea.

But one thing I used to draw on for article ideas was my diary. I've always kept them and they are an invaluable source of ideas and inspiration. They've also helped me when I've been between writing projects and I'm not sure where to go next. The physical keeping of a diary on a day to day basis at least makes you think you are writing regularly and it helps you to manage your thoughts.

You can use them to write about your emotions and feelings in a way that you would never speak them out loud. A diary is a personal, secret companion who you can tell your innermost thoughts to. If you're worried about someone reading it then get one with a lock or hide it in a special place. Your diary can be your best friend, someone you sit with every evening and tell them how your day went and more importantly, how it made you feel. If you don't keep a diary, try using one now for opening up a communication channel with yourself.

A M Dunnewin adds "I love journals. Granted, what I write is usually random thoughts and ideas that are in no way put in order (and sometimes not written consistently), but just the fact that they're down on paper makes me feel somewhat accomplished. Like dropping a heavy load and feeling that weight lift. When it comes to brainstorming, I always turn to pen and paper first. It's like setting a good foundation, while typing is the mad rush to get it all out before the inspiration dies."

Freeflowing Ideas

I'm sure you are aware of freeflow writing when you just take pen and paper, give yourself a time limit and just write down whatever comes to mind. This is usually used in conjunction with working through writer's block to come up with new ideas or to play with a story that has got stuck but you can also use it to help you to work out personal issues.

Take a piece of paper and write down one word that encapsulates your current dilemma then just let your mind flow. Write down anything and everything however random it seems. Then put it away for a few days and come back to it with fresh eyes. In amongst your ramblings, have you addressed the issue? Come up with a solution to your problem? When you let your subconscious flow, it will often flag up a word or phrase that can be useful in dealing with your situation. Pick out those words and freeflow again if the answer is not clear. Each time you freeflow with a related word, your subconscious is digging deeper and deeper to get to the root of your problem and come up with a solution that you hold deep inside.

Creating Dialogue to Deal with Issues

This is a great technique especially for creative writers who so often write down other people's dialogue. I use this when clients come to me and they are unhappy about the way something went in their lives, like a job interview or a meeting with an editor that didn't go so well.

You can rewrite the conversation as you would have liked it to happen. Write out your part and their part. Put into words what you wish you had said. If you felt angry but didn't let them know, disappointed but you held it to yourself, upset by the way things went and wish they had gone differently, then it can help to rewrite the dialogue of that event in a way that empowers you.

This does a few things. One, it boosts your confidence and helps you to see that although that meeting didn't go the way you hoped, future meetings could go a lot differently. Two, it helps you to formulate what you wish you had said. You know the way in which you always think of the best retorts or remarks after the fact? Writing dialogue where you write what you wish you said can give you a sense of satisfaction.

The Power of Poetry

I once attended a poetry workshop with some work mates who had never been to any kind of writing workshop before. It had a mixture of activities but the theme was what it meant to be a woman. After participating in some group exercises, we all found a personal space to sit and write a poem. I looked up at my friend and saw the tears streaming down her face. Writing a poem was opening up a well of emotion within her that was being released and she truly hadn't expected it.

Poetry has the power to open up your thoughts and tap into your inner feelings even if you aren't a poet or rarely dabble with the medium. There's just something about it that delves into our inner thought. It's also believed to be calming and soothing especially if you use rhyme or a particular repeating pattern.

Try writing your own poem to soothe any feelings of turmoil and change. Give yourself a theme – love, work, health, relationships – and just let your words flow. This doesn't have to be a poem for publication, just a poem for you, to help you express what you are feeling. If writing poetry really isn't your thing, try reading some published poets to see how other writers expressed their feelings and dealt with their emotions.

Listen to Your Dreams

I'm a vivid dreamer. I dream full length feature films that I often write down in my ideas' book when I wake up for future use. There are many theories around why we dream and some say it is merely the brain's way of dealing with information it has taken in during the day and is still processing. As we know though, we can dream of past events, access forgotten memories and have the most frightful or scary experiences while we dream. The mind is a hive of imagination that doesn't quiet on sleeping but continues to work. Some theorists have suggested that dreaming is also a way in which your subconscious tries to tell you things, working on issues when you are asleep and helping you to resolve any internal conflicts.

Many people say that they can't remember their dreams but researchers have found that if you concentrate on recalling your dreams in the first few moments upon waking, that they are easier to remember. Keep a notebook by your bedside for these moments and jot down your thoughts even if they seem to bear no weight on your present circumstances. Is your subconscious mind trying to help you out with a solution that your conscious mind hasn't come up with yet?

If not, there are two tips that dream theorists suggest. One is to go to sleep thinking about your situation or issue and ask yourself to come up with a solution. The problem with this is that it might keep you awake all night worrying rather than nodding off and letting your subconscious do the work. The other technique is to be aware of yourself in your dreams so that you can work on your issues subconsciously. Many people don't believe they can do this but it is possible especially if you are a vivid dreamer. It often works best when you are woken in the night or early morning then as you fall back to sleep you remind yourself you are dreaming and you want the solution to your worries. Try to get your dreaming mind to work for you and if all else fails use what you come up with for the basis of stories and writing projects. You'll be in good company – Stephen King often used his dreams for writing inspiration and Mary Shelley came up with the idea for Frankenstein in a waking dream.

Therapy Letters

This is a technique that a psychotherapist once told me to use (yes, I've been there!) for dealing with issues you have with other people that you cannot voice. You basically write them a letter – a letter you will never send – that tells them how hurt, angry, sad or emotional you feel about something you are not happy with that has occurred in your life. It's a great way of really telling that person what you think of them and how they made you feel. It's a release of emotion on paper that gets something that has been preying on your mind out in the open. You then read it a few days later when you aren't feeling quite as emotional about the situation and underline the things that are most important to you. You write a second letter that just deals with those main points, leave it again and go through the process of underlining again until one day when you read that letter you will come to think actually none of this bothers me anymore, I've let it out and now I have nothing left to say to you.

A Letter to the Self

If you know you are susceptible to depression and low moods, you can write a letter to yourself when you are feeling good to be opened when you are experiencing tough times. This letter is a positive reminder that things are not so bad. In it, you write down all your positive attributes, how good you are at writing, what great successes you have had and what you hope for in the future. You give yourself sound advice, like you would a friend, on how to lighten your mood and start feeling good about yourself again. Pin it to your vision board or keep it in a drawer and when you feel like times are difficult, open up your letter of advice to yourself and take note of what you said knowing that things will get better and you will return to the positive place you were in when you wrote your letter.

Taking a Break

Sometimes we just need downtime to give ourselves breathing space and to help us work out what's going on in our lives and where we are headed. When one of my clients came to me saying they were utterly exhausted, I suggested taking a break. They said they had no money for a holiday so that was out of the question. What about just giving yourself a week off? I suggested. What would you do if you had a week to yourself? They came up with visiting the library for a browsing session, going to visit a new museum exhibition, getting through a pile of reading they had been putting off and taking time out to visit friends. A holiday week can work whether you fly away to sunnier isles or stay at home. As writers we work constantly and can forget to give ourselves a break and we all need one at times. My children are no longer in school but I still take time off during school holidays as a way of breaking up my working routine and giving myself time to relax.

Of course, if you have the cash, you can head off for a few days to somewhere new that will enlighten your senses and lift your mood. If you're worried about leaving your writing behind, you can always take pen and paper with you. I go on little side trips that usually involve research.

Writing retreats are a great way to take a break and hook up with other writers. Ok so you'll still be writing but in new and fresh surroundings. It's also a great way of finding out about crossing genres if you take a course or workshop while you are on a retreat. You don't have to pressurise yourself to get x amount of words done. Just go with the holiday flow and you'll be surprised how much a break can improve your writing and lift your mood.

A M Dunnewin says, "When inspiration doesn't strike, I've learned that taking a break from writing is sometimes more necessary than trying to push it. Being out in nature or socializing with friends usually get the juices flowing, though the best trick I found is just listening to music or reading (or sometimes even both). Books and music always does the soul good."

Sarah Zama says, "There are times when I have to stop because my brain won't work.

When this happens, I never force myself to write because I learned long ago that if my head is not there, there's nothing I can do about it. If I force myself, I'll have to rewrite everything anyway. So I prefer to do other things. If I'm just a little tired, I usually do something else, most notably cleaning the house or baking (with a preference for the second). Sometimes I can write later on in the day, sometimes I just wait until tomorrow.

Other time I have to stop. I mean, really stop. One day, two days, one week. Sometimes several weeks. I just let it happen. When this happens, it's because my brain needs rest. I just give it that. I do completely different things; I never force myself to think about my story. It gets back to me when it's time. I naturally start thinking to it again. And yes, when a long time has passed – say a week or two – the temptation to just leave it may be strong, but if you're into your story, when you feel it's time, you'll just sit down and start writing."

Taking a break however long can be beneficial to your writing and give you the rest you need to invigorate and inspire your writing senses so you're ready to start working again when the time feels right.

Turning to Nature

Suzanne Ruthven says, "Environment is a very important stimulus for me and I have to be surrounded by 'Nature' and be able to escape. At the moment it's the mountains of Ireland, which are very productive. An urban working environment doesn't work for me at all."

How many poets have been inspired by Nature? How many writers have sat with a pen and notebook writing descriptions of settings that they see before them? So many of us neglect to see the beauty and wonder of the natural world around us but if we give ourselves a chance to experience being with Nature, it can be a liberating and inspiring experience.

Make a date with the outside world to clear your mind and feel invigorated by the beauty that surrounds you. Head to the beach, the mountains, a forest, a lake – any place of natural beauty and just sit and be in that space. Use your writing senses to notice everything around you, from birdsong to the wind to the animals hiding in the trees to the smell of woodland flowers.

Nature is full of energy and you can use it to refresh your mind and see your path more clearly.

Dusting Down and Clearing Out

Some of us need physical activity to help us work out any problems or issues we are facing. So sometimes procrastination by housework does have a purpose! If you're experiencing a downturn in your writing career, clearing out your writing cupboards and files, your computer and writing space, your boxes, drawers and shelves, can reinvigorate your writing. In between writing books recently, I decided to have a clear-out and found a box file full of stories I'd written years ago; some will probably stay in that box file forever but a few stood out. I'd sent a story into a fantasy magazine who sent it back with feedback that it should be developed as a novel. I forgot that so I dug it out and am thinking, ten years down the line, of actually going for it. I also found a children's story that I was happy with but had done nothing about so I dusted that off, found the old floppy disc it was on and turned it into an e-book. Schazamm! Back in writing mode!

When you spend years writing, you start accumulating half started novels, bits of stories, articles you didn't quite finish and ideas that you wrote notes about but didn't get to proposal stage with. If you've collected these in various places, you can surprise yourself with what you will find when you are dusting down and clearing out. You can use them as a benchmark to see how far you have come and how much your writing has developed. You can turn up old successes that you forgot that you had and comments made by happy editors you could pin on your vision board or writing space wall to give yourself a well-deserved boost.

Reviewing Your Goals

If the tough times you are experiencing are really about your writing then reviewing your goals can help. It could be that you are striving for something that is too big a task and needs chunking down or that a goal you thought was most precious to you is now no longer relevant. Lives change and so do our goals. Just because we have written them down doesn't mean that they are set in stone. They are a plan, a way of organising ourselves and putting down in writing what we hope to achieve but if they become a struggle or they are not producing the outcome that you had hoped for then reviewing and adapting your goals can help you to refocus on your writing life.

I was offered a job as a columnist on a website and it was my goal to write weekly posts that were humorous and would put a smile on people's faces. I loved the idea and wrote many posts upfront so that I could send them in regularly. My other goal was to produce such a portfolio that I would be taken on as a columnist in a big, glossy magazine but within a few weeks the idea was scrapped by the managing editor. All the work I had done was for nothing. There would be no portfolio and no move to a magazine. Columnist jobs are notoriously hard to find unless you are an expert in your field but I thought I had a foot in the door. It was a goal that I had to give up and it taught me a lesson, never do lots of work for a website unless a deal has been struck!

So I went back to my goals and looked at what else I wanted to do and carried on. There will always be other goals to aim for. To help you decide on what to focus on, you can write a 'pros' and 'cons' list. Take each goal and write what would be good about achieving it and what are the more negative aspects of going ahead with that particular project. Lists are great for making you feel organised and they can help you to make decisions about where you are headed and what clutter to clear out of the way so that you can get there.

Seeking Help

At the beginning of this chapter, I said that you can be your own therapist but if things are really not working for you whether in your writing life or your personal life, don't be afraid to seek professional help. I'm not saying that you have to seek a therapist or a counsellor if you don't want to but consider who would be the most appropriate support and look at where you can get help to make the tough times easier. Life coaches and especially creativity coaches can help you to put everything into perspective and balance your writing with the other demands life makes of you. Even checking in with a friend who is a good listener and shares sound advice can give you an outlet for your worries.

One thing my Nan told me when I was going through a bad time was that it will pass. I say this to myself now whenever things get tough and problems seem to be all around me. It will pass. Time will continue regardless of how you are feeling right now. Better and brighter times are just around the corner.

Chapter 9

Ways of Moving Forward

Once you're in a writing flow and know that writing is what you must do more than anything in the world, you need to keep that momentum up; never forgetting for a moment that writing is in your blood and you were made to be creative. This chapter includes ways in which other writers support themselves to keep going because the sky really is the limit no matter how clichéd that may seem. There are always writing opportunities and always ways in which you can grow and develop as a writer.

Maintaining a Writer's Momentum

One way to maintain your momentum is to keep yourself firmly involved in the world of writing. Read the magazines and the new writing books that come out. Look at forums and websites and keep an eye on developments and trends in the publishing world. Go to seminars, attend workshops and conferences. Immerse yourself in all things writing.

I've just had an idea for a screenplay and so I dashed to the library to gather an armful of books for hints and tips, found a lecture series to watch on TV and signed up for some website newsletters to get info on what production companies are looking for. Jumping into a new writing world can really invigorate your writing and support you to channel your energies towards a new project.

I know I've mentioned writing magazines before but one in particular, *Writing Magazine,* is a UK publication that has a Writers' News section in it that is great for maintaining momentum by giving you new ideas of where to send your work, new opportunities that might get your cogs whirring and info on competitions and awards. I have responded to several of these news snippets and seen my work published as a result. Sometimes reading about an opportunity will spark an idea or make you dust off a manuscript that has been sitting in a drawer. It also helps by giving you the will to try something new, making you work to a deadline and explore new possibilities with your writing. Check out what writers' news you can read, whether it's in a magazine or on a website, to keep that momentum going.

You can also surround yourself with people who you can talk to about your writing – if you need to. Whether it's friends you can meet up with, a group you attend or online chats with other writers. Find people who can goad you on and will you to succeed. Even if it's just a friendly editor!

Info Gathering

I'm probably too much of an info gatherer. Like I said, I dashed off to the library to get books on screenwriting but hey, it doesn't cost anything and it opens up your mind to new creative musings. Whenever I have an idea, I scan books, check out websites and load myself up with knowledge about whatever it is that has caught my imagination.

Info gathering isn't just about research. It can be done when you just have the barest glimmer, the slightest idea to go on, but it's a great way of delving into what is out there already and whether your idea has a place to go.

Info gathering can be done when you don't have time to write but are always thinking about your next project. Creative writers do it a lot by picking up bits of people's personalities for characters, interesting names for a protagonist, interesting objects for use in a story. Whatever type of writing is your forte, info gather constantly, using a notebook or just absorbing elements of life that could be turned into some form of writing. Even just making everyday conversation with people you meet can send you off on a tangent that will lead to more info gathering and the momentum to write a new piece of work.

Educating Yourself

In my pursuit to find out more about screenwriting, I watched a lecture given by the great Guillermo Arriaga, writer of *21 Grams* and *Babel*. He was like a breath of fresh writing wisdom. He doesn't believe in rule books or writing to a rigid structure. His point of view intrigued me and gave me much food for thought.

You can maintain momentum by educating yourself and listening to other people who have achieved their goals. Try attending one-off lectures or workshops. If you want to really study in greater depth, think about returning to college or university. There are some great BA and MA degree writing courses available these days and if you can't physically attend them then there are many more writing courses online.

Even experienced writers who have a few successes under their belts should consider whether they would enjoy a course with feedback provided by other professionals. This can work especially well if you want to cross genre and are unsure of your abilities. It's easier to send your work to a tutor for correction than it is to just take the plunge in a new area of work. I recently took a distance learning scriptwriting course and it really gave me the new skills and motivation to produce something in this area. I've now applied for a place on an MA in English with Irish Literature but then I love learning and am always doing some course or the other because I believe that we should never stop learning and opening ourselves up to new knowledge.

Think of ways in which you can educate yourself. Personal and professional development is a lifelong process and what you learn can help you to move forward as a writer.

Online Support

The Internet has opened up many possibilities to writers including the chance to talk to other writers and get online support.

Joe Griffin told me, "I have some friends who are writers and sometimes we share our experiences, and I check in on writing blogs and Twitter accounts to make contacts and remind myself that I'm not alone."

Amanda J Evans says, "My main support is my family and friends but I also like to participate in some of the groups on the internet. I am a member of quite a few groups on LinkedIn and I subscribe to a number of writing blogs and newsletters too. I also use social networking."

Melinda Feeney and Sarah Zama both use Critique Circle (www.critiquecircle.com), a web-based Internet critique group. Melinda says "I have been in a group called Critique Circle for just over a year now. It has proven to be the single most important thing I have done in regard to my writing. What I have learned from the good people there has improved my writing tenfold. It's amazing what you don't know when you don't even know you don't know!"

Sarah adds "I'm a member of an online workshop, the Critique Circle. Have been for five years now. I enjoy it a lot. I'm a non-native English speaker, and in the workshop I found the support to my learning the language – and learn it with the purpose of writing fiction – that I always wanted and never found. But I also learned a lot about the art of writing. I met quite a few fantastic people and some of them are not only writing buddies now, but real friends.

I also learned to take critique without fearing it. Yeah, sure, receiving a crit from a stranger is always a peculiar experience, but now I just read it and take what good there is. Something good or interesting is always there. And I just enjoy my friends' crits. Receiving them is always a pleasure, whatever they have to say about my story."

Networking

Niall McArdle uses his contacts and friends for support, "I have several friends who I rely on for feedback, and when I'm ready to hear what they have to say, I email them pages. It's always terrifying. They are all brilliant readers, and each has different strengths and interests, so you end up getting interesting perspectives. They're not emotionally attached to it, so their comments can seem cruel at times, but they are looking at it as readers, not as the person teasing the story out from the writing gods. I don't know what I would do without those emails from those people. I used to belong to a writers' group, but I had to leave because it stopped being a writers' group and started turning into group therapy. I wasn't interested in hearing people's personal problems; I have enough of my own. Going to author readings is also inspiring. Not the reading bit, which is usually awful – it's called prose for a reason – but the discussion afterwards. It's good to know that even an established, successful author can feel like a total loser sometimes. It gives me hope."

Create networks of like-minded people to support you through the tough times, to celebrate with during the good times and to remind you that you are a writer when doubts surface or you're in between projects.

Writing Groups – Yes or No?

Writers have divided opinions about writing groups. Some like Niall have tried them; others don't feel comfortable in a group setting or don't have one to attend locally. They aren't everyone's idea of networking but for some writers they do provide a vital support.

Jennifer Burke, an aspiring novelist based in Ireland, wouldn't be without her group. Jennifer told me, "My biggest support – and I feel it has significantly affected the quantity and quality of my writing – is a writing group. I've been writing for as long as I can remember (literally!) but without knowing any other authors. I took a couple of courses in the Irish Writers Centre and while the courses themselves were very useful, my favourite part was meeting other aspiring writers. I couldn't believe there were so many out there, all struggling along in their bedrooms with their laptops, just like me.

When I put one of my novels forward for the Irish Writers Centre's Novel Fair Competition, one of the other entrants emailed us all about starting a weekly writing group, just for the purposes of finalising our books for the competition. While fifteen people turned up on day one, only seven or eight stuck it out on a regular basis. When the competition was over, we decided not to disband the group.

We now meet once a month. We all email part of our work to the group the week before our sessions. At the meetings, we read out our pieces and everyone gives feedback. The best part about the group is the range of genres, including women's fiction, fantasy, science fiction, crime, general fiction and humour. The scope is inspiring and I learn as much from critiquing others' work as I do from the advice I am given (which is often extremely helpful – a fresh pair of eyes is worth ten re-writes). Having first met seven months ago, we are now very comfortable with each other and no one takes negative criticism as anything other than constructive. We stick strictly to the timetable to ensure everyone's work gets a fair hearing, but we punctuate the meetings with casual conversations about how we're keeping motivated and our general writing lifestyles.

I find I push myself to write more every month to ensure I have good quality work to show the group at the next meeting. I look forward to our sessions immensely because it is my only chance to meet with other writers. I had a short story published last year about a woman who killed her husband. Some non-writer friends who read the story were surprised by the content, having expected that my stories would reflect my own life. I think they were concerned that I was hiding some dark secret! This serves as an example of why I need the group. They understand writing and imagination.

I take every piece of critique I receive from the group on

board. I do not always make the changes they suggest but I do consider every point and I firmly believe my writing in general has improved because of the feedback. If the group ever disbands, I will be devastated. Internet sites, blogs and forums are interesting, as are self-help books. But nothing beats actual personal contact with other writers and, if I ever become a famous writer and am asked to give advice to aspiring authors, it will be: *join a writing group.*"

If there isn't a writing group in your locality but you would like the support of a group, consider starting your own. Ask around and see if there are other writers nearby who would be willing to join and share their expertise and stories. Stick an ad in your local paper or on the supermarket notice-board. It doesn't matter how many members you get. If there are enough people to share their work and a room you can use to gather in, you have the makings of a group that can be a valuable support.

Keeping Your Creative Mind Active

There are numerous ways in which to keep your creative mind active. Ok I have to admit here that I love my little Nintendo DS. I'm not a games fan in general but I love word games, brain training exercises, crosswords and logical problems. It's something to do in the evening when your brain is still active but you've run out of words for the day.

I recently read about a writer that loves Scrabble and crosswords and gives himself a break by doing a quick game on the computer. The Internet has a wealth of word games and puzzle sites that you can explore in your downtime. There are also sites that give you creative prompts so that if you find yourself between projects and you need to flex your creative muscles, you can find something on the web to kick start new thought processes.

Any writer should have on their shelves a few books like *The Creative Writing Handbook* by John Singleton and Mary

Luckhurst, *Life-Writes* by Suzanne Ruthven or *The Creative Writer's Handbook* by Cathy Birch. Books that give you ideas, exercises and prompts so that if you feel like trying something different or, if you need a break away from your main writing project, you can do something else to keep your creative mind active.

One of my clients goes to the theatre or to the cinema, not just to enjoy a night out, but to analyse how plays and films work. She looks for audience reactions – what makes people gasp in horror? Laugh at the same time? When do they feel tension? What endings do they come away talking about? It's her way of analysing the best points of screen and playwriting with a view to informing her own work but it's not as strenuous as a writing session.

What ways can you use your creative mind to support your writing but have fun doing at the same time?

Coaching Others

If you have lots of experience and something to share with other writers, think about coaching or mentoring beginner writers. Many writers support their income by tutoring students for colleges, universities and online writing schools. But could you take it a step further? Make yourself available as a coach or consultant?

If you have access to an office space or have a home office, you could consider taking on clients and charging for your services. There are some great home study courses that you can take to learn the basics of life coaching or NLP and combined with your writing skills, you could be helping other writers to tap into their creative potential and overcome any obstacles that life throws at them.

There are so many people who start writing but need the support to get to a finished product. Often when I mention that I'm a writer, someone will say they have started a book or would love to write their memoirs or have this amazing idea for a story but they just need the encouragement to see their goals realised. Being a coach or consultant can help many aspiring writers to achieve their goals and often it is just having someone to talk to who has been there and done that that can spur them on to becoming a published writer too.

You can also move forward by helping out in your local community. Community groups love guest speakers and writers who will host workshops for them. I've worked with women's groups and active age groups to help them produce books or to get them started on their own personal writing projects. You might not get paid a fortune but giving something back to the writing community is ultimately rewarding and to be able to have helped others fulfil their writing dreams is a pleasure in itself.

Taking an Active Role in a Writer's Organisation

Many of us have subscriptions to organisations, guilds or societies. Is there a way you could become more involved? Like taking a position on their board or heading a regional group? Talk to the organisations you are involved in to see in what ways you could take a more active role. If you don't have the time to be a permanent member of the board, you might be able to help out in other ways. Is there an event that needs organising? Or a competition that needs judges? Think about offering your services to societies that support writers and sharing your skills and expertise with your fellow men and women. As you move forward in your writing career, help others to move forward in theirs too.

Chapter 10

Resources for the Writer's Mind

If you're stuck for inspiration or just fancy a browse, check out some of these resources for writers.

Websites for Writers

You probably have a list of writers' websites that you visit regularly but you might find something else here to whet your appetite!

- A Book Inside: How to Write and Publish a Book: www.abookinside.blogspot.com
- Ask about Writing: www.askaboutwriting.net
- Author: www.author.co.uk
- Author-Network: www.author-network.com
- Drew's Script-O-Rama: www.script-o-rama.com
- Evil Editor: www.evileditor.blogspot.com
- E-Writers: www.e-writers.net
- Fiction Writers Connection: www.fictionwriters.com
- Inky Girl: www.inkygirl.com
- International Thriller Writers: www.thrillerwriters.org
- Literary Mama: www.literarymama.com
- Mystery Writing Is Murder: www.mysterywritingismurder.blogspot.com
- Plays On The Net: www.playsonthenet.com
- Poets and Writers: www.pw.org
- Romance Junkies: www.romancejunkies.com
- Screenwriters Online: www.screenwriter.com
- The Irish Writers Centre: www.writerscentre.ie
- Writers Net: www.writersnet
- Writers Reign: www.writersreign.co.uk

- Writer Unboxed: www.writerunboxed.com

Organisations

Here a just a few of some of the many writers' organisations around the globe.

- Association of Authors and Publishers: www.authorsand-publishers.org
- Australian Society of Authors: www.asauthors.org
- Crime Writers Association: www.thecwa.co.uk
- Historical Writers Association: www.thehwa.co.uk
- Horror Writers Association: www.horror.org
- International Women's Writing Guild: www.iwwg.com
- National Union of Journalists: www.nuj.org.uk
- Science Fiction Writers of America: www.sfwa.org
- The Association of Authors Agents: www.agentassoc.co.uk
- The Authors Guild (USA): www.authorsguild.org
- The British Fantasy Society: www.thebritishfantasysociety.co.uk
- The Society of Authors: www.societyofauthors.org
- The Society of Indexers: www.indexers.org.uk
- The Writers Guild of America: www.wga.org
- The Writers Guild of Canada: www.writersguildofcanada.com
- The Writers Guild Of Great Britain: www.writersguild.org.uk
- Writers Union of Canada: www.writersunion.ca

Writing Courses

There are so many courses available nowadays on all different writing genres that it's worth browsing to find the course that best suits you. Check out how many assignments you will need to complete, whether the course is certified, who your tutor will be and see a sample of the course materials before you make a decision.

- Chrysalis – The Poet in You: www.lotusfoundation.org.uk
- Creuse Writers Workshop and Retreat: www.creusewritersworkshopandretreat.com
- Fire in the Head: www.fire-in-the-head.co.uk
- Literature Training: www.literaturetraining.com
- London School of Journalism: www.lsj.org
- National Council for the Training of Journalists, UK: www.nctj.com
- Open College of the Arts: www.oca-uk.com
- Swanwick Writers Summer School: www.swanwickwritersschool.co.uk
- The Arvon Foundation: www.arvonfoundation.org
- The Big Smoke Writing Factory: www.bigsmokewritingfactory.com
- The Publishing Training Centre: www.train4publishing.co.uk
- The Writers Academy: www.thewritersacademy.net
- The Writers Bureau: www.writersbureau.com
- Writers News Home Study Courses: www.writers-online.co.uk/home-study

Writing Prompts

If you've stuck and need inspiration, give one of these creative sites a try.

- Creative Writing Prompts: www.creativewritingprompts.com
- Creativity Portal: www.creativity-portal.com/prompts/imagination.prompt.html
- Easy Street Prompts:

www.easystreetprompts.blogspot.com
- Plinky: www.plinky.com
- The Story Starter: www.thestorystarter.com
- The Writers Block Online:
  www.thewritingblockonline.com
- Toasted Cheese: www.toasted-cheese.com
- Writing Fix:
  www.writingfix.com/classroom_tools/dailypromptgen
  erator.html

Critique Sites

Try out a new piece of work with other writers and see what feedback and constructive criticism you get. You can also critique other people's work and share some of your knowledge at one of these sites.

- Authonomy: www.authonomy.com
- Critique Circle: www.critiquecircle.com
- Ladies Who Critique: www.ladieswhocritique.com
- My Writers Circle: www.mywriterscircle.com
- Review Fuse: www.reviewfuse.com
- Scribophile: www.scribophile.com
- The Desk Drawer: www.winebird.com
- Writing : www.writing.com

Word Games

Every writer deserves some downtime! Take a break and have some fun with these online word games.

- East of the Web: www.eastoftheweb.com
- Fun with Words: www.fun-with-words.com
- Gamehouse: www.gamehouse.com
- Games: www.games.com
- Shockwave: www.shockwave.com

- Word Games: www.wordgames.com
- Word Games: www.wordgames.net
- Wordplays: www.wordplays.com

Competitions

Get your brain working to a deadline with one of these competitions.

- Acorn Independent Press Crime Novel Competition: www.acornindependentpress.com
- Aesthetica Creative Works Competition: www.aestheticamagazine.com
- BBC National Short Story Award: www.bbc.co.uk/nssa
- BBC Wildlife Nature Writer of the Year award: www.discoverwildlife.com
- Betty Trask Prize and Awards: www.societyofauthors.org
- British Haiku Awards: www.britishhaikusociety.org.uk
- Bulwer-Lytton Fiction Contest: www.bulwer-lytton.com
- Crime Writers Association Debut Dagger Award: www.thecwa.co.uk
- Debut Quarterly Competition: www.parkpublications.co.uk
- Eric Gregory Award: www.societyofauthors.org
- Fish Competitions: www.fishpublishing.com
- Mslexia Women's Short Story Competition: www.mslexia.co.uk
- NaNoWriMo: www.nanowrimo.org
- RTE Radio Short Story Competition: www.rte.ie/radio1/francismacmanus
- Sentinel Annual Poetry Competition: www.sentinelpoetry.org.uk
- The British Fantasy Society Short Story Competition: www.britishfantasysociety.org
- The N.A.W.G Open Short Story Competition:

www.nawg.co.uk
- The New Writer Prose and Poetry Prizes: www.thenewwriter.com
- WF and FG Froud Annual Children's Short Story Competition: www.scpsw.co.uk

Events

Fancy a day out? Here are a few of the more well-known festivals that are held in the UK. Check out local listings for what's on in your own locality wherever you are in the world.

- Bath Festival of Children's Literature: www.bathkidslitfest.co.uk
- Birmingham Book Festival: www.birminghambookfestival.org
- Borders book festival: www.bordersbookfestival.org
- Cambridge Wordfest: www.cambridgewordfest.co.uk
- Chester Literature Festival: www.chesterfestivals.org.uk/literature
- Dundee Literary Festival: www.dundeeliteraryfestival.co.uk
- International Playwriting Festival: www.warehousetheatre.co.uk
- Kings Lynn Festivals: www.lynnlitfests.com
- Literature Wales: www.literaturewales.org
- London Literature Festival: www.southbankcentre.co.uk
- N.A.W.G Festival of Writing: www.nawg.co.uk
- PULSE International Poetry Festival: www.thesouth.org.uk
- The Festival of Writing: www.writersworkshop.co.uk
- Winchester Writers Conference, Festival and Bookfair: www.writersconference.co.uk

Social Media

Link with many writers and other professionals in the publishing industry, using:

- Facebook: www.facebook.com
- Twitter: www.twitter.com
- LinkedIn: www.linkedin.com
- Pinterest: www.pinterest.com

Promoting Your Work

Get your profile on these sites and use them to promote your work.

- Filedby: www.filedby.com
- Goodreads: www.goodreads.com
- Library Thing: www.librarything.com
- Litopia Writer's Colony: www.litopia.com
- Red Room: www.redroom.com
- Scribd: www.scribd.com

Further Reading

Life Coaching and NLP

Making your Creative Mark by Eric Maisel

The 12 Secrets of Highly Creative Women by Gail McMeekin

Co-active Coaching by Laura Whitworth, Karen & Henry Kimsey-House and Phillip Sandahl

Coaching with Spirit by Teri-E Belf

Coaching with NLP by Joseph O'Connor and Andrea Lages

The Life Coaching Handbook by Curly Martin

The Essential NLP Practitioners Handbook by Murielle Maupoint

Writing Guides

A Practical Guide to Poetry Forms by Alison Chisholm

Creating Convincing Characters by Nicholas Corder

Handy Hints for Writers by Lynne Hackles

Horror upon Horror by Suzanne Ruthven

How to Write a Chiller Thriller by Sally Spedding

How to Write a Romance Novel by Susan Palmquist

How to Write and Sell Great Short Stories by Linda M James

How to Write for the How-To Market by Suzanne Ruthven

Life-Writes by Suzanne Ruthven

So You Want to be a Freelance Writer? by Deborah Durbin

Telling Life's Tales by Sarah-Beth Watkins

The Author's Guide to Publishing & Marketing by Tim Ward and John Hunt

The Country Writer's Craft by Suzanne Ruthven

The E-book Writer's Guide & Directory by Susan Palmquist

The Lifestyle Writer by Sarah-Beth Watkins

The Pagan Writer's Guide by Suzanne Ruthven

The Positively Productive Writer by Simon Whaley

The Writer's Group Handbook by Julie Phillips

The Writer's Internet by Sarah-Beth Watkins
Unlock Your Creativity by Sue Johnson and Val Andrews
Write a Western in 30 Days by Nik Morton
Writing a Stand-Up Comedy Routine by Jenny Roche
Writing and Selling Travel Features by Solange Hando

Contacting the Author

You can find me on the web or on Facebook, Twitter and LinkedIn. Alternatively, drop me a line at:

- watkinscoaching@gmail.com.
- Website: sarahbethwatkins.wordpress.com
- Facebook: www.facebook.com/SarahBWatkinsWriter
- Twitter: @SarahBWatkins
- LinkedIn: Sarah-Beth Watkins

You can also look up more about Compass Books and John Hunt Publishing on:

- Compass Books: www.compass-books.net
- Facebook: www.facebook.com/JHPCompassBooks
- John Hunt Publishing: www.johnhuntpublishing.com

Contributors

Meadhbh Boyd

Bread and buttered in County Clare, Meadhbh is an Ethnomusicology graduate of the School of Music and Theatre, UCC. Since moving to London in 2011, she has enjoyed a varied career in the arts and media – with a focus on content-making and creative development. She has contributed as a writer on Big Brother (C5, 2012), performed for the Turner Prize nominated piece, Tino Sehgal: These Associations (Tate Modern 2012), read aloud her LOL-packed teenage diary at CRINGE London (2013) and tours, records and composes extensively as a fiddle player and performer. Currently working as a barista, and Creative Producer for musical comedy, Laundrette Superstar, with writer Fortuna Burke. She loves a good shot of java and hates when people smile awkwardly when you enter the loo cubicle after them! Contact Meadhbh@meadhbhboyd or www.meadhb-hboyd.com.

Jennifer Burke

Jennifer Burke is a Dublin based author of two (as yet unpublished) contemporary fiction novels and is currently working on her third. As a member of the Irish Writers Centre, Jennifer has completed a number of courses, including Finish Your Novel with Conor Kostick in 2012. Jennifer attends a monthly novel writing group and also writes shorter fiction. Having been shortlisted in the 2012 From the Well Competition, she had her short story published in the resulting anthology. Jennifer was also shortlisted in the Fish Publishing Flash Fiction Competition in both 2012 and 2013.

A M Dunnewin

A. M. Dunnewin inherited her love for mysteries and thrillers from her family, which helped her pursue a BA in Psychology with a minor in Criminal Justice. Although her stories cover a wide range of genres, she primarily writes historical fiction and thrillers. An avid reader at heart, she's also a passionate collector of both antique books and graphic novels. She lives in Sacramento, California.

Deborah Durbin

Deborah Durbin has spent the past 16 years doing her dream job – getting paid to write. Having tried a succession of 'proper jobs' and failing miserably at all of them due to her inability to be told what to do (of the 30 jobs she's had, she's walked out of 29 of them), she qualified as a journalist and now spends her days writing content for lots of glossy magazines, along with writing books as and when a subject comes to mind. She is the author of 11 non-fiction books and two novels. Her latest book, So You Want To Be A Freelance Writer?, is now available. Deborah doubts very much that she will have a 'proper job' again.

Amanda J Evans

Amanda is a professional freelance writer, author, ghostwriter, poet and spiritual teacher living in Ireland. Amanda is the author of two non-fiction books. *From Those Death Left Behind* is a personal account of the effects of suicide on her family and the struggle to survive and overcome the destruction that such a death leaves behind. *Messages From The Angelic Realms* is a collection of inspirational messages received during meditation. These messages instil hope, compassion and motivation and help those who read them to look at life in a different way.

She is currently working on a fiction novel in the young adult area. This is a fantasy novel that includes magic, a dark lord, battles against evil and more. Find her at www.amanda

jevans.com.

Melinda Feeney

Mother of three, wife, recently retired strategy consultant for a major online recruiting company. Melinda has been writing for about 10 years and only within the last year considered publishing anything. She's a complete seat-of-your-pants type of person. No blog. Little social media. Just stories to tell and the will to tell them.

She comes from an oral culture (Mohawk Nation) and this reflects in her writing. Her characters are mainly minorities, alternating between being like everyone else and struggling with unique circumstances because of their racial/political affiliations. Strong characters and dialogue drive all her stories.

Her WIP is a romance, set in Puerto Rico where two children, thrown together through tragedy spend their entire lives looking to fill the emptiness those tragedies caused when they discover the answer lies in each other. It will be ready for publication by fall 2013.

Joe Griffin

Joe Griffin is a well-known writer, journalist and presenter who writes fiction as well as features, reviews, opinion pieces and profiles on all areas of popular culture. He has just completed his first novel and as a journalist his work has been published in Ireland, England, The United States and Australia. Joe has written for over a dozen outlets on the subjects of cinema, videogames, music, literature, comedy, lifestyle, tech, television and more. He has written for The Irish Times, The Guardian, The Irish Independent and The Sunday Times, regularly appears on Arena on RTÉ Radio 1 and has contributed to shows on BBC, TV3, Today FM, Newstalk and Phantom.

Marilynn Hughes

Marilynn Hughes has three children and had a career in broadcasting as a news anchor, reporter and producer. Marilynn has experienced, researched, written and taught about Out-of-Body Travel and Mysticism since 1987 and has appeared on innumerable radio and television programs to discuss her thousands of out-of-body experiences. She is featured in the documentary film 'The Road to Armageddon' which was released in 2012 and has been included in 'The Encyclopedia of the Unseen World,' (By Constance Heidari, Red Wheel Weiser) in 2009. Marilynn founded 'The Out-of-Body Travel Foundation' in 2003 and has written 75 books, 40 magazines and around 15 CDs on Out-of-Body Travel and Comparative Religious Mysticism. Marilynn is a former Feature and current Contributing Writer for Suite101.com's International Magazine and Online Encyclopedia. Find her at www.outofbodytravel.org.

Krystina Kellingley

Krystina is a reader and commissioning editor/copy editor/publisher of imprints Axis Mundi Books (esoteric books), Cosmic Egg Books (Fantasy/Sci Fi/Horror), Our Street Books (children's books) and Dodona Books (divination). She has just had her first children's book, *Mistflower – The Loneliest Mouse*, published and is currently working on an adult supernatural fiction novel. She has had several short stories published in spiritual magazines as well as many online articles on dream interpretation and other subjects. As well as teaching creative writing, she has worked as a hypnotherapist, counsellor and a dream analyst. Krystina travels internationally to tutor in writing workshops as well as privately mentoring new writers of adult and children's fiction. She has a BA in Imaginative Writing and Literature and an MA in Creative Writing. She lives in the UK.

Niall McArdle

Niall McArdle is an Irish writer based in Canada. His fiction has appeared in Phoenix Irish Short Stories. He has had work published in The Irish Times, The New Orleans Review of Books and The Malahat Review. He is the author of a critical study of Roddy Doyle. He is currently writing a novel, collecting rejection letters from The New Yorker and waiting for Uma Thurman to return his calls.

Anna McPartlin

In the early nineties, Anna ran an alternative cabaret called Tales of the City in a run down bar on Capel Street, Dublin. The show comprised of a Dutch torch singer, a folk rock band, an ancient alcoholic queen of monologues, and a waitress in drag... not to mention comedy. Anna was a stand up comedienne for four years and it is her experience writing sketches that ignited her passion for storytelling.

Anna's debut novel *Pack Up The Moon* was published in January 2006, it went on to be a best seller both at home and abroad. Since then Anna's written three more novels, *So What If I'm Broken* being her latest work. She's also written *School Run*, a TV comedy-drama for TV3 which was nominated for both an IFTA and a TV award. Anna's books are published in Ireland, Germany, America, Russia, The UK and Australia. She's currently working on her first film. More about Anna can be found on her website www.annamcpartlin.com

Nik Morton

Nik Morton served in the Royal Navy as a Writer, and then went into IT. He has sold over 120 short stories, hundreds of articles and edited several books and magazines. Now 'retired' in Spain, Nik contributes reviews, articles and artwork to magazines in Spain and the UK. In the early 1970s, Nik completed a Writing Correspondence Course and was so successful that he was asked to become a tutor; unfortunately, his career precluded taking this on. Nik has sold articles on writing and run workshops for novel writing and scriptwriting. He has been chairman of several Writers' Circles. Nik is married to Jennifer; they have a daughter, Hannah and a son-in-law Farhad (Harry), and grandson Darius, who have also moved to Spain. In February 2011, he was hired as the editor-in-chief of the US publisher, Solstice Publishing.

Writing as Ross Morton, Nik has 5 western novels published: *Death at Bethesda Falls, Last Chance Saloon, The $300 Man, Blind Justice at Wedlock* and *Old Guns,* and a western e-book, *Bullets for a Ballot.* Writing as Nik Morton, he is the author of the crime thriller *Pain Wears No Mask* and two psychic spy Cold War thrillers *The Prague Manuscript* and *The Tehran Transmission,* a collection of 21 crime short stories that feature Leon Cazador, Spanish Eye, "a perfect TV vehicle for Antonio Banderas," he says! He's also the author of a modern vigilante crime thriller, *A Sudden Vengeance Waits,* an anthology in aid of Japanese earth-quake/tsunami survivors, *When the Flowers are in Bloom,* and a vampire horror-crime thriller, *Death is Another Life,* which he's also written as a screenplay. As Robin Moreton, he's the author of a World War I erotic thriller – *Assignment Kilimanjaro.* He's also the editor of A Fistful of Legends, 21 stories of the Old West.

Nik's website is: www.freewebs.com/nikmorton and his blog can be found at http://nik-writealot.blogspot.com

Suzanne Ruthven

Former editor of The New Writer, in partnership with literary agent, Merric Davidson, Suzanne started her professional writing career in 1987 by founding the small press writers' magazine Quartos, which ran for nine years until its merger with Acclaim in 1996 to become TNW. Author of over 20 titles on spiritual, country-lore and self-help matters (including two novels) she has regularly contributed freelance articles to a variety of publications as diverse as The Lady and the Funeral Director's Journal.

In 1994 she founded ignotus press to market and promote new authors in the increasingly popular Mind, Body & Spirit area, and for over 10 years the press was recognised as one of the leading publishers in the metaphysical genre; remaining so until her retirement and move to Ireland in 2005. She has also ghost-written numerous books for other writers in the metaphysical, country and folk-lore genres, including an autobiography for one of Britain's leading field sportsman. Currently commissioning editor for Compass Books (an imprint of John Hunt Publishing), she now lives in Ireland with her partner and nine greyhounds... and a little mongrel called Harvey. Suzanne's blog can be read at www.suzanneruthvenatignotuspress.blogspot.ie

Lawrence Wray

Lawrence Wray has written several short stories and a novel which are all available on Amazon. He spends his time between working in his own business during the day and writing at night in bed instead of reading – well that was the idea – but always ends up reading into the wee small hours anyway.

He is currently working on a novel about a guy with cancer which is based on his own experience but with a bit of humour included.

Sarah Zama

Sarah Zama has been a bookseller in Verona (Italy) for eight years. She has been writing since the age of ten and has published fantasy short stories for children and adults in magazines and anthologies both in Europe and the USA. After a hiatus of a few years, she is now back to writing. She has completed an old project (a fantasy novel for children) and she's now working on a trilogy of urban fantasy novels set in Chicago during the Prohibition era.

**COMPASS
BOOKS**

Compass Books focuses on practical and informative 'how-to' books for writers. Written by experienced authors who also have extensive experience of tutoring at the most popular creative writing workshops, the books offer an insight into the more specialised niches of the publishing game.